Essential
Turkey
West Coast

by Sean Sheehan

An experienced travel writer, Sean
Sheehan has contributed to guide books
to many European and Asian destinations.
Essential *Turkey–West Coast* is his
second AA Essential Guide, his first being
Essential Bali & Lombok. Formerly an
English teacher in the Far East he now
divides his time between homes in Ireland
and London.

Above: *inviting beaches draw the crowds to
Turkey's West Coast*

AA Publishing

A fisherman on the island of Bozcaada prepares his catch

Front cover: *Turkish farmer; Ölüdeniz; local carpet*

Find out more about AA Publishing and the wide range of services the AA provides by visiting our web site at www.theaa.co.uk

Written by Sean Sheehan

Produced by AA Publishing
© The Automobile Association 1999
Maps © The Automobile Association 1999

Distributed in the United Kingdom by AA Publishing, Norfolk House, Priestley Road, Basingstoke, Hampshire, RG24 9NY.

A CIP catalogue record for this book is available from the British Library.

ISBN 0 7495 1922 3

The contents of this publication are believed correct at the time of printing. Nevertheless, the publishers cannot be held responsible for any errors or omissions or for changes in the details given in this guide or for the consequences of any reliance on the information provided by the same. Assessments of attractions, hotels, restaurants and so forth are based upon the author's own experience and, therefore, descriptions given in this guide necessarily contain an element of subjective opinion which may not reflect the publisher's opinion or dictate a reader's own experience on another occasion.

We have tried to ensure accuracy in this guide, but things do change and we would be grateful if readers would advise us of any inaccuracies they may encounter.

Published by AA Publishing, a trading name of Automobile Association Developments Limited, whose registered office is Norfolk House, Priestley Road, Basingstoke, Hampshire, RG24 9NY.
Registered number 1878835.

Colour separation: Pace Colour, Southampton
Printed and bound in Italy by Printer Trento srl

Contents

About this Book

KEY TO SYMBOLS

✚ map reference to the maps found in the What to See section

✉ address or location

☎ telephone number

🕐 opening times

🍴 restaurant or café on premises or near by

🚌 nearest bus/tram route

🚆 nearest train station

🚢 ferry crossings and boat excursions

ℹ tourist information

♿ facilities for visitors with disabilities

✋ admission charge

↔ other places of interest near by

❓ other practical information

➤ indicates the page where you will find a fuller description

---

Essential *Turkey: West Coast* is divided into five sections to cover the most important aspects of your visit to Turkey's west coast.

Viewing Western Turkey pages 5–14
An introduction to Western Turkey by the author.
    Western Turkey's Features
    Essence of Western Turkey
    The Shaping of Western Turkey
    Peace and Quiet
    Western Turkey's Famous

Top Ten pages 15–26
The author's choice of the Top Ten places to see in western Turkey, each with practical information.

What to See pages 27–90
The two main areas of western Turkey, each with its own brief introduction and an alphabetical listing of the main attractions.
    Practical information
    Snippets of 'Did you know...' information
    4 suggested walks
    4 suggested tours
    2 features

Where To... pages 91–116
Detailed listings of the best places to eat, stay, shop, take the children and be entertained.

Practical Matters pages 117–24
A highly visual section containing essential travel information.

Maps

All map references are to the individual maps found in the What to See section of this guide.

For example, Bodrum Kalesi has the map reference ✚ 59B1 – indicating the page on which the map is located and the grid square in which the ancient castle in Bodrum is to be found.

A list of the maps that have been used in this travel guide can be found in the index.

Prices

Where appropriate, an indication of the cost of an establishment is given by **£** signs:

£££ denotes higher prices, **££** denotes average prices, while **£** denotes lower charges.

Star Ratings

Most of the places described in this book have been given a separate rating:
✪✪✪   Do not miss
✪✪   Highly recommended
✪   Worth seeing

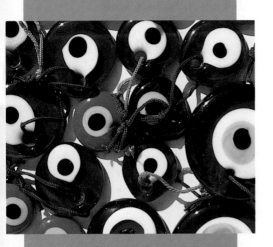

Viewing
Western
Turkey

Above: *the lucky eye, protection against malign influences, is common in Turkey*
Right: *hand-painted dolls from Alanya are a colourful example of Turkish craftwork*

Sean Sheehan's Western Turkey

The calm waters of Ölüdeniz, though banned to yachts, are ideal for cruising in smaller craft

Beaches lapped by turquoise water, rocky crags carpeted with pine trees that look down on olive groves, blue and white beehives set out on bare rocks, sunseekers relaxing on white sand beaches, antique fishing villages and ancient civilizations – the images of Turkey in the travel brochures are based on fact, and they only hint at the richness of the Aegean coast of Turkey. The major resorts are Kuşadası, Bodrum and Marmaris, with Fethiye and Ölüdeniz not far behind. Here and elsewhere, Turkey receives tens of thousands of holidaymakers each year, yet still manages to preserve its traditional, and legendary, regard for hospitality and friendliness. Turkish people are convivial and curious, homely and hospitable to a fault, and for many visitors the lasting impression they have of the country is not the food, the beaches or the ancient sites, but of the straightforward friendliness of the people they have met.

Few destinations can match western Turkey's capacity to fulfil the disparate needs of so many different kinds of visitors. If you want to dance and party till 5AM and sleep in until the late afternoon then Bodrum and other resorts are waiting to receive you. If Greek and Roman art is more to your liking then Ephesus is just one of the many incredibly well-preserved sites waiting to be explored. Best of all, do both and find time for everything else in between.

Getting Around

Public transport in western Turkey is a dream. Coaches, buses, *dolmuşes* and minibuses go to virtually every place of interest. Very few destinations require you to use a taxi or private car. Organised tours to major sites are readily available but you can almost always reach them easily on your own.

Western Turkey's Features

Geography
• Turkey's west coast stretches south from Çanakkale to merge with the Mediterranean off Patara some 500km south as the crow flies. The waters of the Çanakkale Boğazi (Dardanelles) (➤ 38) are a traditional dividing line between Europe and Asia, which makes most of western Turkey a part of Asia. The Romans regarded the region as Asia and, until quite recent times, it was generally referred to as 'Asia Minor'.

People
• The population of western Turkey is remarkably homogeneous. Nearly everyone is ethnically Turkish and the non-Muslim proportion of the population is around just 1 per cent.

Religion
• Virtually everyone is a Muslim, nominally at least, and mosques are commonplace, but the secular aspect of Turkish society is more obvious along the western Turkish coast than anywhere else in Turkey.
• Elsewhere in Turkey, the month-long religious festival of Ramadan (➤ 116) transforms daily life, but holidaymakers on the western Aegean coast may not even notice it is happening. Western dress and manners are commonplace.

Surprises
• Turkey is the world's only secular Muslim democracy, the second largest European force in NATO, and the only production centre outside the US for the F-16 warplane. Women received full suffrage in 1934. Turkey has more private TV stations than any other country in Europe.

East meets West
Western Turkey is a fascinating mixture, with elements of both the Middle East and Western Europe. Turkey has applied to join the European Union, but both the Turkish people and the decision-makers in Brussels seem more uncertain about Turkey's place in Europe than ever before.

Both Muslim minarets (below), and pagan temples, like the one at Assos (bottom), form part of Turkey's rich culture

Essence of Western Turkey

A boat ride and a stroll through classical ruins are two popular activities when visiting western Turkey

Western Turkey is steeped in 5,000 years of dramatic history, and is intoxicating for anyone with an interest in the origins of European civilisation. It started here – not in Athens or Rome – when Greek colonists sailed across the Aegean to the coast of modern Turkey and established settlements that would nurture the first known historians, geographers, philosophers and poets. Many inspiring ruins of this cradle of European culture still stand, alongside resort hotels, sandy beaches, watersports facilities, and discos that belt out dance sounds as the sun rises over Homer's Troy.

THE 10 ESSENTIALS

If you only have a short time to visit western Turkey, or would like to get a really complete picture of the area, here are the essentials:

• **Venture into a *hamam*** (Turkish bath) and experience the bath of a lifetime, followed by an invigorating massage on the stone platform built over the oven that heats up the water (➤ 115).

• **Explore one of the Greek or ancient Roman theatres**, many of which are remarkably well preserved, built with stone into the hillside (➤ 19, 26, 52).

• **Cruise the Aegean**, if only for a day, from Bodrum, Marmaris or Fethiye, in a traditional *gület*. Bathe on an otherwise inaccessible beach and swim in the crystal-clear water (➤ 61, 72).

• **Watch the sun set over Çanakkale Boğazi (the Dardanelles)**, the narrow strait that separates Asia from Europe and has inspired lovers, poets and generals, often with tragic consequences (➤ 38).

• **Relax and talk** with Turkish people over a glass of tea or a game of backgammon in the street and discover their friendliness and sense of hospitality.

• **Enjoy Turkish *meze*** (appetisers, ➤ 97) with fresh bread, washed down with a glass of *raki* (➤ 98).

• **Visit Efes (Ephesus)**, Rome's renowned Asian capital where a quarter of a million citizens lived. Today it is one of the world's best-preserved ancient cities (➤ 19 and 41–43).

• **Go snorkelling or scuba diving**: Bodrum, Kuşadası and Marmaris are all good centres for both.

• **Go shopping in a bazaar** and be prepared to get lost: İzmir's is especially labyrinthine (➤ 104).

• **Party till dawn** at Bodrum's Disco Halikarnas (➤ 114) or one of the many other nightspots.

Above: *the carefully restored Library of Celsus at Efes (Ephesus)*

Below: *fun and frolics on the beach at Ölüdeniz*

9

The Shaping of Western Turkey

2500–2000 BC
Bronze Age settlement at Troy (➤ 55), reflecting the development of trade in the Aegean and the emergence of rich and powerful local rulers.

1200 BC
The Greeks raze Troy, inspiring Homer's *Iliad*. In real life, the sack of Troy was probably the culmination of economic rivalry between peoples in the Aegean. Around this time, Ionians and Greek colonists begin arriving on the Aegean coast and establish settlements such as Miletos, which later become the cradle of European science and philosophy.

900–334 BC
The kingdoms of Caria, Lycia, Lydia and Phrygia emerge and govern different areas of western Turkey. Lydia, ruled by King Croesus (561–46 BC) at Sardis, invents coinage, but unwisely takes on the Persians and the capital is sacked. Under Miletos, Ionian cities rise in rebellion against the Persians, but to no avail. The Persians cross the Dardanelles (➤ 38) to Greece itself but are soundly defeated. In 334 BC Alexander the Great re-establishes Greek culture along the coast.

This Hellenistic Age is characterised by intense economic and cultural activity.

AD 44–330
St Paul encounters paganism at Ephesus, (➤ 19). Western Asia Minor has been part of the Roman Empire since 133 BC; in the 2nd century AD Ephesus becomes the Romans' regional capital and flourishes. In AD 330 Constantinople (Istanbul) becomes the capital of the eastern Roman empire, known as the Byzantine Empire.

1250
Commercial ambitions lead the Genoese to expand in the Black Sea and south into the Aegean. Many Aegean islands become independent Genoese principalities.

1451–1566
The Turkish Ottomans under Mehmet II capture Constantinople and rename it Istanbul. It becomes the capital of their Empire which extends to Syria, Mesopotamia, Egypt and parts of eastern Europe and North Africa. Ottoman rule reaches its height under Süleyman the Magnificent, who captures Rhodes in 1522 and Bodrum in 1523 from the Knights of St John.

Ottoman male dress from the early 19th century

1683
The limit of the Ottoman Empire is reached when the siege of Vienna fails for a second time.

1800s
Ottoman power declines as the European Great Powers are relied on to keep the Russians out.

1853–56
The Crimean War increases reliance on Western powers.

1908
The 'Young Turks' rebel against the sultanate and foreign intervention.

1914–1919
Turkey allies itself with Germany in World War I, and fiercely defends the

Dardanelles at Gelibolu (Gallipoli, ➤ 44) in the northern Aegean. In 1918 Turkey accepts humiliating peace terms, and the Ottoman Empire comes to an end. In 1919 the Greek army occupies İzmir and moves inland.

1919–1923
In the War of Independence (1919–1922), the Turks defeat the Greeks, who retreat to İzmir, committing atrocities along the way and abandoning the Greek inhabitants to reprisals: İzmir is partly destroyed. Greece and Turkey agree to an exchange of populations, and the Turkish Republic is declared. Mustafa Kemal (known as Atatürk, father of the Turks) begins to westernise Turkey and make it a secular state.

Turkey's most revered leader, Atatürk, is commemorated throughout the country

1980s
The Turkish coast draws Western Europeans in search of simplicity, sun and sea. Backpackers are drawn to quaint fishing villages that later develop into the major resort towns. Hotel construction on a large scale begins.

1990s
Islamic parties challenge Turkey's secularism. In 1998 the Islamic Welfare Party succeeds in banning casinos but the Welfare Party itself is outlawed for threatening the secular basis of Turkish society. The military repression of Kurds in the southeast of Turkey continues unabated.

Peace & Quiet

In resorts such as Bodrum, where the discos and bars only *begin* to get lively around midnight, the prospects for peace and quiet may seem slim indeed. Yet even the big resort areas have secluded spots within reach. Bodrum is an ideal base from which to explore the coast and islands by boat, and the Bodrum peninsula itself is rugged in parts, and relatively unspoilt.

Bird Life
Reserves such as the Dilek Milli Parkı have the most species but you will see birds almost everywhere. Storks build their immense nests on tall buildings; eagles, buzzards and vultures soar overhead. On walks through agricultural land anywhere along the coast look for the crested lark on the soil and, overhead on telephone lines, colourful bee-eaters and blue rollers. The wild flowers are fantastic too.

In the northern Aegean the Dilek Milli Parkı (➤ 40) is only 30km south of Kuşadası. To make the most of this national park it helps to have your own transport. Within the park, you can climb Samsun Dağı (1237m), from the village of Eskidoğanbey (preferably not in the summer months) – a wonderful way to see wildlife and landscape. Further away from the main resorts, the Kuşcenneti National Park, just south of the Sea of Marmara, is a fantastic place for birdwatching (➤ 49).

Near Selçuk and accessible by public transport, the formerly Greek village of Şirince lives up to its name ('pleasantness') and makes a good base for a walk amidst peach and apple orchards in the surrounding hills. Further south, use the resort of Fethiye (➤ 68–9) as a base for exploring quiet villages tucked away in the countryside, but near the coast. If you are touring outside the high season, it should not be difficult to find inexpensive accommodation in a *pansiyon* (such as Anita & Ned's ➤ 102), with home-cooked food and family hospitality.

In the Northern Aegean, the islands of Gökçeada (➤ 45) and Bozcaada (➤ 37) are quiet and feel very remote from the more developed parts of the Turkish Aegean. Bozcaada is smaller, but is best for solitary country walks and near-deserted beaches.

Bafa Gölü (Lake Bafa)

This bird and wildlife area became a Nature Park and National Park in 1994. A good accommodation base would be the village of Kapıkırı, near ancient Herakleia (➤ 45). Some of the *pansiyons* here can arrange guides for trekking expeditions into the hills (➤ 100). For general information, write to PO Box 18, Bebek, 80810 Istanbul ☎ 0212 281 0321; fax 0212 279 5544.

Right: you can get away from the crowds
Inset right: *sunset over Bafa Gölü (Lake Bafa)*
Above: *a short-toed eagle*

Western Turkey's Famous

Reading Homer
Both the *Iliad* and the *Odyssey* would be appropriate reading on a visit to western Turkey, and there are numerous translations to choose from. In the 1960s Richard Lattimore translated both books in verse form and in 1990 another American, Robert Fagles, brought out an acclaimed new translation of both works. The translations are available in paperback.

The great historian Herodotus grew up in one of the many colonies established on the Aegean coast of modern Turkey

Homer (c8th century BC)

Homer's epic poems, the *Iliad* and the *Odyssey*, are the foundation stones of European literature. Homer's birthplace is most likely to have been Smyrna, now the modern city of İzmir. Strabo, who hailed from Tralles (Aydın, ► 35), writing his *Geography* in the 2nd century AD describes a shrine and statue of the poet erected in the city. Virtually nothing is known about Homer, and even his existence has been disputed, but it is now generally agreed that the *Iliad* and *Odyssey* were compiled from older compositions in the second half of the 8th century BC. The *Iliad* tells the story of the seige of Troy (► 55), which lasted for ten years, until the Greeks entered the city with the help of guile and a wooden horse. The *Odyssey* recounts the adventures of Odysseus as he struggles to make his way home after the war.

Herodotus (c490–c425 BC)

The 'father of history' was born at the start of the 5th century BC in Halicarnassus (Bodrum, ► 58). He travelled

extensively, not only along the Aegean coast, but also in Greece, Egypt, Persia (Iran) and parts of Italy. The subjects of his *Histories* are the wars between Greece and Persia, and along the way he provides fascinating information about the kingdoms that ruled Asia Minor before the Persians arrived on the scene. He was particularly fascinated by the Lydians and their fabulously rich king, Croesus, whose capital was at Sardis. In one of his anecdotes Croesus has been captured by the Persian king Cyrus, and asks what the Persian soldiers are doing to Sardis. 'Plundering it', smirks Cyrus, 'and confiscating all your wealth.' Croesus replies, 'Not mine, my friend, it is your wealth now that they are stealing,' whereupon Cyrus brings the plundering to a quick finish.

Top Ten

Above: *the theatre at Hierapolis can be explored in detail*
Right: *the famous statue of Artemis from Ephesus*

1
Aphrodisias Stadium

S30C2

40km southeast of Nazilli, off the main Aydın–Denizli road

Summer 8–7; winter 8–5:30

Restaurants (£–££) in Karacasu, 13km to the west

Dolmuş/minibus from Karacasu or Nazilli

None

Aphrodisias (► 34)

Tours from Kuşadası and other resorts

Stadiums adorn many of Turkey's ancient sites but none can compare with the one at Aphrodisias, which is the best-preserved example of its kind.

The word 'stadium' comes from a measurement of about 200 metres, the distance of the shortest foot race in ancient Greece and which over time came to be used for the public arena where races and other games took place. The stadium of Aphrodisias stretches for just over 263m and its 25 rows of seats could accommodate 30,000 spectators. Its excellent state of preservation owes a great deal to the Turkish professor Kenan Erim, and his team at New York University, who effectively resurrected Aphrodisias between 1961 and his death in 1990. The stadium had been buried as a result of earthquakes in the Middle Ages and from the 13th century onwards the whole of Aphrodisias had been abandoned and more or less forgotten about by the world.

It is best to follow the path that leads round the site, going first to the theatre and then to the Odeon and Temple of Aphrodite on the right. A little way past this the path heads north for 200 metres to reach the spectacular stadium. The Romans were keen to emulate the Greek tradition of holding sporting and artistic competitions to mark religious festivals and the impressive scale of this stadium shows what importance was attached to public entertainment. The stadium was the scene of a major festival and sporting competitions, and as well as the traditional Greek events – foot races, wrestling, boxing and pentathlon – the Romans also had chariot races and gladiatorial combats.

The stadium at Aphrodisias was unseen for centuries until archaeologists unearthed the entire site

2
Bodrum Kalesi
(Castle of St Peter, Bodrum)

This grand example of 15th-century crusader architecture dominates Bodrum harbour and houses the Museum of Underwater Archaeology.

| Bodrum's harbour is dominated by the castle on its rocky promontory

The Knights Hospitallers of St John, militant anti-Muslim Christians, arrived in Bodrum in 1402 and set about choosing a site for a mighty fortress. The first of its double curtain walls was completed in 1437 but building work continued until 1522; shortly thereafter the Knights were forced to evacuate because Süleyman the Magnificent captured their headquarters in Rhodes. In the outer courtyard there is an impressive collection of amphoras (storage pots) recovered from offshore wrecks, like most of the museum's collection of artefacts. Inside the main castle there were separate towers for the English, French, Italian and German contingents, each proudly displaying its own coat of arms.

The Glass Wreck Hall (separate admission charge) contains a carefully preserved 7th-century Byzantine trading ship – one of the oldest preserved shipwrecks in the world – alongside its cargo of glass. The Carian Princess (separate admission charge) is named after the royal resident of a sarcophagus that was discovered in 1989. The English Tower has been restored in a mock-medieval style. Armour and trophies decorate the walls, and staff in medieval costumes sell glasses of wine.

Climb to the top of the castle, above the Carian Princess room, for wide views of Bodrum and the harbour. The more morbid will enjoy the dungeons, restored and embellished with ghoulish scenes and sound effects.

59B1

Bodrum, behind the tourist information office

(0252) 316 2516

8:30–12, 1–5 (longer hours in Jul and Aug). Closed Mon

Cafés (£) inside the castle

Limited access. Video-show room for disabled visitors

Cheap to moderate, depending how many sections are visited

Bodrum (➤ 58–62)

17

3
Çeşme

The resort town of Çeşme has preserved its Turkish heritage

A low-key, relaxing resort on the coast, with Ottoman architecture and thermal springs, Çeşme has managed to avoid the worst excesses of tourism.

✚ 30A3

✉ 80km west of İzmir

🕓 Castle and museum 8:30–12, 1–5:30. Closed Mon

🍴 Restaurants (£–££) along the seafront

🚌 *Dolmuş*/minibus from İzmir

⛴ Greek island of Chios, 9km offshore

ℹ Near the pier
☎ (0232) 712 6653)
🕓 Jul–Sep, Mon–Fri 8:30–7; Oct–Apr, daily 8:30–12, 1–5

♨ Castle and museum cheap

↔ İzmir (➤ 31–3), Sigacik (➤ 54)

Many of the houses close to Çeşme's seafront are well-preserved homes from the 19th century, and an evening wander through the streets is very rewarding. The word *çeşme* (pronounced chesh-ma) means 'fountain', and a number of old Ottoman fountains still exist in the town. People come to Çeşme for its water: there are therapeutic thermal springs in the area and you can benefit from these at some of the local hotels. Delightful decorated balconies adorn many of the Ottoman buildings, and there are two 18th-century mosques. A 14th-century Genoese fortress dominates the town, and is now home to a small, uninspiring museum.

Çeşme is not as blatantly touristy as resorts like Bodrum and Kuşadası, but the town has still developed a modest entertainment infrastructure for visitors. Any of the agencies dotted around town can arrange a day trip to Hĝos (Chios), and a longer trip to Italy via Brindisi is also possible. There is a Turkish bath in the centre of town, and although Çeşme itself is quiet at night, the surrounding area has a number of lively discos (➤ 113) and pubs (➤ 112). Ilica, just 4km to the east, is the liveliest place for evening entertainment and also boasts the best beach in the vicinity. The beach at Boyalık is more exposed, but hot springs in the seabed help compensate for any chill in the air.

4
Efes (Ephesus) Theatre

This great Roman theatre had seating for 24,000. From the top row there is an unsurpassed view of ancient Ephesus.

A detail from the decoration behind the stage at Ephesus

In the AD 60s a real life drama was played out here when St Paul's preaching sparked off an anti-Christian demonstration (Acts 19:24–41). A pagan silversmith named Demetrius accused the Christians of disrespect for the goddess Artemis and a riot broke out. Paul left shortly afterwards, leaving Demetrius and others to recover their trade in Artemis merchandise. Their successors may be seen peddling Artemis memorabilia in the many stalls that line the entrance to Ephesus.

In classical Greece, theatres had no stage: all the action took place in the orchestra. In Hellenistic times a small stage was introduced, and the Romans doubled this in size to some 6m in depth. Hence the decorated double row of columns and single row of pilasters, which are still standing – they once supported the stage.

From the stage area, with its various entrances, it is obvious how the steepness of the auditorium gradually increases, to provide good views for those in the cheaper seats at the back. In the auditorium itself, listen to people talking in the stage area: the acoustics are still excellent, though the Greeks and Romans also placed bronze and clay sounding boards at strategic spots. From the higher rows there is a superb view of the road now known as the Arcadian Way. The reedy grass at its far end indicates what was once the line of the harbour.

✚	30B3
✉	3km from Selçuk
☎	(0232) 892 6402/892 6940
⏱	8–6:30 (5:30 in winter)
🍴	Restaurants (not recommended) at the Lower Entrance. Bring a picnic or eat in Selçuk (► 53)
🚌	Buses to Selçuk from Kuşadası and İzmir
ℹ	(► 53)
♿	None
✋	Cheap
↔	Selçuk (► 53), Meryemana (► 50), Kuşadası (► 46–7)
❓	Tours from most resorts

5
Hierapolis

30C3

Pamukkale, 19km north of Denizli

Museum 9–12, 1:30–5. Closed Mon

Motel Koru (➤ 70) and restaurants (£–££) near the museum

Dolmuş/minibus from Denizli, long-distance bus from Marmaris, Kuşadası, Fethiye and other towns

Opposite the museum
☎ (0258) 272 2077
🕐 8–12, 1:30–7:30 (1:30–5 in winter)

None

Cheap

Pamukkale (➤ 22–23), Laodiceia (➤ 49)

The huge theatre at Hierapolis is a dramatic statement in its own right

Roman architecture on a grand scale dominates Hierapolis. The theatre is vast, and the necropolis was one of the biggest in Asia Minor.

The King of Pergamum (➤ 24), Eumenes II, developed Hierapolis in the 2nd century BC, but the monuments that attract visitors today were constructed by the Romans after they inherited the town. The name means Holy City, and the town was associated from the start with the mysterious Springs of Pamukkale close by (➤ 22–3). To appreciate the scale of the Roman theatre, take a seat in the very top row. Then go down into in the theatre orchestra, which gives access to the fine reliefs behind the stage. The lower ones can be admired at close quarters.

After leaving the theatre, if time permits, turn to the right and continue up the unpaved track to pass remains of the city walls, before turning left for the ruins of the Martyrion of St Philip. If time is limited, head back to the car park from the theatre and turn right to reach the colonnaded Frontinus Street. This splendidly preserved Roman street begins just after the Motel Koru on the other side of the road. Frontinus Street is 4m wide and at the north end has a monumental gate, dedicated to the emperor Domitian in AD 84. As you walk towards the Domitian Arch look out for the well-preserved Roman public toilets on the right. Continue through the Domitian Arch to the large necropolis, dotted with lavish tombs. The Roman baths now contain a museum.

6
Ölüdeniz

The soft, sandy beach, with a backdrop of pine-covered forests, is over 3km long, and the water in the lagoon is transparent – but avoid high season.

The name of Turkey's most beautiful beach setting means 'dead sea', referring to the calmness of the water, which is almost completely cut off. Ölüdeniz is a warm, sheltered lagoon that manages to be magnificent, despite the lack of a view of the open sea. At the height of summer it is packed with people; out of season, there is little that can compare. The setting is superb: the beaches stretch for such a distance that it is usually possible to find some space, though not so easy during a summer's weekend. The most picturesque stretch of beach winds around the lagoon but is closed off and requires a separate entrance fee. This pay beach proves more popular with Turkish families, while other holidaymakers favour the long stretch of Belcegiz.

Despite the popularity of Ölüdeniz, successful efforts have been made to preserve the pristine beauty of its waters. Yachts are forbidden to use its sheltered location, and an attempt has been made to contain the most rampant hotel development. Hotel advertising boards spoil the approach to Ölüdeniz from Fethiye, and the surrounding area is heavily developed. The protected water of the lagoon is ideal for safe canoeing and kayaks are readily available for hire. At night, there is plenty of opportunity for partying at nighspots in nearby Ovacik and Hisarönü, but the food scene is dismal, despite the proliferation of restaurants. Take a picnic lunch if going for the day.

🕆 30C1

✉ 15km south of Fethiye

🍴 Restaurants (£–££) fronting the beach

🚌 *Dolmuş*/minibus from Fethiye

♿ None

✋ Pay beach (cheap)

↔ Fethiye (► 68–9)

The beauty of Ölüdeniz is no longer a secret

21

7
Pamukkale

🕇 30C3

✉ 19km north of Denizli

☎ (0258) 261 3393

🍽 Motel Koru (➤ 70) and restaurants (£–££) near the museum

🚌 *Dolmuş*/minibus from Denizli, long-distance bus from Marmaris, Kuşadası, Fethiye and other towns

The spring pool that attracted the Romans is now part of a motel. Swim here amongst the submerged columns of an ancient portico.

Hot spring water cools as it comes to the surface on the edge of a plateau, some 100m above the Lycos valley, and as the dissolved calcium bicarbonate gives off carbon dioxide, the remaining calcium carbonate solidifies. The prosaic chemistry does scant justice to the place: what it means is that the water runs down a series of bright white terraces of precipitated chalk formed into irregular pools, odd shapes and stalactites.

From the valley below, you see the high plateau swathed on one side with white cliffs. Hence the name Pamukkale, or 'cotton castle'. The ancient town of Hierapolis developed because of the springs, which were considered holy, and the Romans established a health spa. So many visitors have followed in their footsteps that measures have belatedly been taken to protect the natural formation. Signs forbid paddlers to wear shoes in the pools, but there are obvious signs of deterioration in the terraces.

Stay a night to take in the strange beauty of the

The calcified waterfalls of Pammukale form a remarkable natural phenomenon

place as evening falls. The Pamukkale Motel is just of one of the many undistinguished hotels but its pool is truly remarkable, containing a collection of fallen masonry from ancient Hierapolis (➤ 20). Get here early to enjoy the experience before the afternoon tour buses arrive and disgorge a flood of visitors, all wanting to take a dip.

🛈 Opposite the museum
☎ (0258) 268 6539/ 272 2077 ⏰ 8–12, 1:30–7:30 (1:30–5:30 in winter)

♿ None

✋ Cheap

↔ Hierapolis (➤ 20), Laodiceia (➤ 49)

❓ Tours combining Pamukkale and Hierapolis from most major resorts

Left: *it's difficult to resist taking a dip in the historic and therapeutic waters*

8
Pergamum

The dramatically steep acropolis at Pergamum has 80 rows of seats

The two great attractions here are the acropolis, a majestic statement of political might, and the Asklepeion, devoted to the art of healing.

30B4

Acropolis: 6km north of Bergama. Asklepeion: 2km south of Bergama

Acropolis and Asklepeion; summer, 8:30–7 ; winter, 8:30–5:30

Restaurants (£) in Bergama

Buses to Bergama from Ayvalık and İzmir

☎ (0232) 633 1862
Summer, daily 8:30–7; winter, Tue–Sun 8:30–12, 1–5:30

None

Cheap

Bergama (➤ 37)

Pergamum emerged as a powerful force in Hellenistic times but the last king, Attalus III, was so keen to placate the Romans that he bequeathed the kingdom to Rome in 133 BC. It remained an important city and today there is plenty to see. An organised tour that includes transport and a guide is worth considering because the acropolis is 8km from the Asklepeion, and both sites contain several points of interest. Otherwise, take a taxi from one site to the other and invest in a specialist guide book (➤ 89).

On the acropolis, the Greek theatre is unusually steep, with 80 rows of seats carved into the hillside. Post holes to the rear of the orchestra still show where temporary scenery was erected as a backdrop to the drama. The partly restored Temple of Trajan evokes the grandeur of the site under the Romans but its art treasures, the relief carvings on the Temple of Zeus, were moved to the Pergamon Museum in Berlin in the 19th century.

At the far end of the modern town of Bergama, the Asklepeion was the leading medical centre of the ancient world. Patients slept in the sanctuary, hoping to be cured by divine influence, and had their dreams interpreted by priestly physicians who prescribed baths in the sacred water that still flows here. The remains of a circular temple to Zeus are worth seeing, and there is a small, well-preserved theatre in the northwest corner. In the southwest corner are remains of the public latrines.

9
Rock Tombs, Fethiye

*The ancient Lycian people left tantalising traces.
When an earthquake flattened Fethiye in 1957,
the Lycian rock tombs remained intact.*

Fethiye stands on the site of the Lycian port of Telmessos. All that remains of the ancient town is its tombs, cut into the rock overlooking Fethiye. Try to visit near sunset when the climb up is less exhausting and when there is the bonus of panoramic views. Steep steps lead up to the most impressive site, the Tomb of Amyntas, a temple-like structure with twin Ionic columns between two pilasters adorned with rosettes at the top. A fading inscription on the left pilaster records that the tomb belonged to Amyntas, and gives the name of his father. Nothing else is known about the family or the 4th-century BC building. The main chamber has a door with four panels, which still have their original iron studs, although tomb robbers have broken in at some time in the past. The iron studs are imitations of the bronze nails which adorned the wooden porches of Greek temples.

✚ 30C1

✉ Fethiye

🕐 8:30–sunset

🍴 Restaurants in town (£–££) and a café (£) opposite the entrance

🚌 Buses to Fethiye from Bodrum, Denizli, İzmir, Marmaris, Pamukkale, Patara

ℹ️ (▶ 69)

✋ Cheap

↔️ Fethiye (▶ 68–9)

The Tomb of Amyntas is an impressive sight

10
Xanthos
Harpy Tomb

30C1

Just north of Kınık, 63km from Fethiye

May–Oct, 7:30–7; Nov–Apr, 8–5

Café (£) across the road but best to bring a picnic

Dolmuş/minibus from Fethiye or Kalkan

None

Cheap

Xanthos (➤ 90), Letoön (➤ 77), Kalkan (➤ 75), Pınara (➤ 85), Tlos (➤ 88), Sidyma (➤ 88)

The ruins of the Roman theatre and the Harpy Tomb in the background (right) alongside a twin sarcophagus

British 'archaeologists' took two months in 1842 to pillage Xanthos of its art treasures, but the site is still capable of stirring the imagination.

Start your visit to this ancient city by taking a seat in the Roman theatre, and gazing down on the orchestra, which is still full of fallen masonry from the stage and its columned façade. The experience evokes an impressive feeling for the history of the site.

To the west of the theatre stand two Lycian pillar tombs, the Harpy Tomb (480 BC) and, alongside it, a twin sarcophagus. The bas-relief at the top of the 5m-high pillared Harpy Tomb carries plaster copies of the marble originals, now in the British Museum. They show seated figures receiving gifts, with bird-like, winged women carrying children in their arms on the north and south sides. These images were once thought to represent the mythical creatures known as Harpies, hideous winged monsters, personifying hurricanes and tornadoes (in Greek the word means 'snatcher'). Modern theories tend to suggest, however, that they are actually carvings of the Sirens, part women, part birds, who lured seafarers to their deaths with their enchanted singing. Here they are carrying away dead souls, in the form of children. The, adjacent, twin sarcophagus dates from the 3rd century BC. It is not known why the tombs were put on top of each other in this unusual manner.

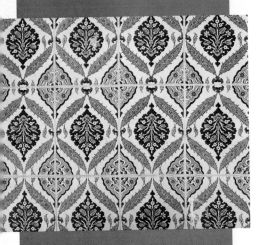

What to See

Visitors to the west coast are welcomed by Turkish people

Northern Aegean

There is so much to see. The chief resort is Kuşadası, one of the liveliest anywhere along the Turkish coast and well placed for day trips to major sites such as Ephesus, Pamukkale and Hierapolis. The city of İzmir (ancient Smyrna) is attractive though somewhat hectic. It is a good place in which to experience the urban Turkish culture that resort towns lack. İzmir is also a convenient base for a visit to the idyllic Temple of Artemis near the site of ancient Sardis, home to the fabulously rich Croesus in the 6th century BC. To the north of İzmir is ancient Pergamum, easiest to visit on an organised tour. Further north again lies the town of Çanakkale, which overlooks the Dardanelles, prominent in history and mythology. The battlefields of Gallipoli are just across the water, and Homer's Troy is just a short day trip away inland.

> *'Three and four times happy*
> *shall those men be hereafter*
> *Who shall dwell on Pagus*
> *beyond the sacred River'*

Advice from the oracle of Apollo after
Alexander the Great suggested
founding the new city of Smyrna

———————●———————

Village life retains a healthy indifference to tourism

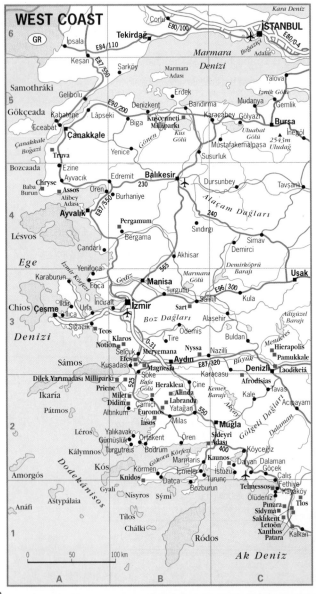

İzmir (Smyrna)

The third largest city in Turkey, home to nearly 3 million people and twinned with Cuba's Havana, İzmir has a long and illustrious past. Homer (▶ 14) is said to have lived here in the 9th century BC. The town was destroyed by the Lydians and lay in ruins for over 300 years, but it came back to life when Alexander the Great founded a new city on the summit of Mount Pagus.

🚩 30B3
ℹ️ 418 Atatürk Caddesi
☎ (0232) 422 0207

Modern İzmir's heyday was in the 19th century when the city was both a major trading port and a cosmopolitan meeting place for merchants from the East and West. It became the focal point of the Greek–Turkish struggle in the War of Independence that followed World War I. When the Turkish army took the city in 1922 the Greek area was set on fire and three-quarters of İzmir burnt to the ground. What the visitor sees today is a very modern metropolis, with a very Turkish bazaar that should not be missed (▶ 33). Two museums give a good introduction to the city's ancient and more recent past (▶ 32 and 33). Another tangible reminder of the past is Mount Pagus, where Alexander the Great was resting after a hunt when a goddess descended and urged him to found a new city. From the top of the hill there is a dramatic view of the city and the great sweep of a bay that continues to make İzmir the major port on the Aegean.

Bottom: İzmir is a large, modern city, but its old quarter (below) is worth exploring

What to See in İzmir

AGORA ⭐

✚ 30B3
✉ 816 Sokak
☎ (0232) 425 5354
⏰ Summer 8:30–5:30;
winter 9–12, 1–5
♿ None
✋ Cheap

The Roman agora (market place) was built by Emperor Marcus Aurelius, after an earthquake in AD 178 had destroyed the original one founded by Alexander the Great. A Corinthian colonnade is the main focus of interest, and items discovered here are on display in the Archaeological Museum.

ARCHAEOLOGICAL MUSEUM ⭐⭐

✚ 30B3
✉ Bahri Baba Park
☎ (0232) 484 8324
⏰ Tue–Sun 8:30–12:30,
1:30–5:30
🍴 Café (£) in the museum
♿ None
✋ Cheap

Greek and Roman statues, monuments and parts of friezes found in and around İzmir fill this excellent purpose-built museum. There are large examples of Roman funerary monuments downstairs, but the more interesting pieces of art are on the ground and upper levels. The examples of Greek archaic art include a fine *kore* (a maiden), while Hellenistic art is represented by a statue of Eros.

ETHNOGRAPHIC MUSEUM ⭐⭐

✚ 30B3
✉ Bahri Baba Park
☎ (0232) 484 8324
⏰ 8:30–12, 1–5:30. Open all
day during high season
♿ None
✋ Cheap

The first floor includes examples of domestic Ottoman architecture, a reconstructed old pharmacy, a display on the making of blue beads for warding off the evil eye, and exhibits on the art of camel wrestling and rope-making. The second floor has a reconstructed Ottoman bridal chamber, a 19th-century living room, a circumcision room and displays of carpets and weapons.

KONAK ⭐⭐

✚ 30B3
♿ Pedestrianised
✋ Free
❓ Bazaar closed Sun

An ancient mosque in the heart of İzmir

This central square near the seafront is the most attractive corner of the city. It has an ornate clock tower, presented to the city in 1901 by the Sultan, and opposite stands a delightful little mosque, enlivened by the ornate enamelled tiles. İzmir's two main museums are just a short distance up the hill and the bazaar is also close by.

Old İzmir

Start outside outside the main tourist office, having picked up a town map.

Turn left and after passing the Hilton go straight ahead at the first junction, walking down Gazi Osmanpaşa Bulvari. After 500m turn left down Sokak 920, at the black-on-yellow sign for the Agora (▶ 32). From the Agora, return to the main road and go back the way you came but on the other side of the road. After about 100m turn left down Sokak 929. At the T-junction at the end turn left onto Anafartalar Caddesi.

This is the main artery running through İzmir's bazaar (▶ 104). There are plenty of side-streets to explore, and it is easy to lose your sense of direction amidst the crowds.

After walking down Anafartalar Caddesi for about five minutes, look for a Y-junction near a dilapidated-looking mosque on the right. Bear left at the junction, signposted Anafartalar Caddesi 1-791, and at the end enter the plaza-like square of Konak (▶ 32). Leave the square the way you came and take the first right turn, by a fountain, into Mıllıkutuphane Caddesi.

At the end of this street the Efes pub is on the right and, opposite, are İzmir's two best museums (▶ 32). You can reach the top of Mount Pagus from here by taking the No.33 bus to Kadifekale.

People live and work at Kadifekale on top of Mount Pagus

Distance
5km

Time
3–6 hours, depending on museum visits

Start point
Tourist Office, 418 Atatürk Caddesi ☎ (0232) 422 0207
🚌 30B3
🚌 63, 114, 118 (from train station), 53,61,257 (from bus station)

End point
Konak bus station
🚌 30B3

Lunch
Efes pub (£)
✉ 7 SSK Işanı, Konak
☎ (0232) 484 7036

What to See in the Northern Aegean

ALİNDA ❂

This little-visited ancient site has impressive ruins, and the setting, on the steep eastern slopes of Mount Latmus, is delightful. Alexander the Great came here and helped the Queen of Halicarnassus (Bodrum ➤ 58–62), then in exile, regain her throne in 334 BC. The chief ruin is a huge and remarkably well-preserved market building. Higher up, the small theatre is overgrown but has also survived well. It is worth seeking out for an unrivalled view over the village of Karpuzlu and the pretty valley formed by the river Çine Çayı. Higher still is a well-preserved watchtower, surrounded by tunnels, partly open, that lead down the hillside.

APHRODISIAS ❂❂❂

This ancient site was associated with fertility cults from as early as the Bronze Age, and the Greeks named it Aphrodisias after their goddess of love, Aphrodite. A temple dedicated to her stood here in the 8th century BC. The Romans transformed Aphrodisias into a major cultural centre, and held sculpture competitions: sculptors were especially attracted to the place because of the quality of local marble.

Parts of the site are periodically closed off for restoration work, but enough is always left open to make a visit rewarding. There is a stadium (➤ 16), a well-preserved Roman theatre, the Baths of Hadrian complete with floor tiles, and the Temple of Aphrodite, which survived its conversion into a basilica during the Byzantine era. Leave time to visit the museum with its extensive collection of sculptures found here.

ASSOS ❂❂

The ruins of the city of Assos stand on a cliff above the pretty fishing port of Behramkale. Founded by Greek colonists in the 8th century BC, Assos was so renowned as an intellectual centre that the philosopher Aristotle lived here for three years. The town was later captured by his pupil, Alexander the Great. The highlight is the partly reconstructed Temple of Athena (530 BC) with its spectacular view of Lesbos, the starting point of the original Greek colonists. There are also very well-preserved sections of the 4th-century BC city walls, over 12m high in places, and a necropolis with an assortment of sarcophagi. The severe-looking mosque by the side of the site dates back to the 14th century. It is well worth wandering through Behramkale to admire the fine old Ottoman bridge, built with stone from the ancient site. There are hotels to suit most budgets, and an overnight stay is worth considering. The local beach is pebbly but clean.

🏨 Hotel restaurants (£–££) in Behramkale

🚐 Dolmuş/minibus from Ayvacik (not to be confused with Ayvalık)

♿ None

💷 Cheap

↔ Chryse (► 38)

AYDIN ⭐

Known in ancient times as Tralles, Aydın today is a busy provincial town with little of intrinsic interest. It is a useful transport point, however, if you want to catch a *dolmuş* east to Nyssa or south to Alinda. If you have time to spare it is worth taking a look in the small archaeology and ethnology museum, west of the park and square that forms the centre of town. Also near the park is an interesting 17th-century mosque. The bus station is over half a kilometre south of the town centre, just off the main road.

✚ 30B3

✉ 50km east of Kuşadası

🏨 Restaurants (£)

🚐 Dolmuş/minibus from Kuşadası, Pamukkale, Selçuk and İzmir

ℹ Just east of the bus station ☎ (0256) 225 4145 🕐 8:30–5

♿ None

↔ Nyssa (► 51), Alinda (► 40)

Fishing boats moored in the pretty fishing port of Behramkale, below clifftop Assos

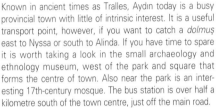

🔝 30A4

✉ About halfway between Çanakkale and İzmir

ℹ On quayside ☎ (0266) 312 3158 🕒 May–Sep 9–1, 2–7,

🍴 Restaurants (£–££)

🚍 *Dolmuş*/minibus from Çanakkale, Assos, Bergama, İzmir

↔ Bergama (➤ 36), Pergamum (➤ 24)

Below: *the Roman Red Basillica in Bergama*

🔝 30B4

✉ 100km north of İzmir, 50km southeast of Ayvalık

🍴 ➤ 92 (£–££)

🚍 Buses from Ayvalık and İzmir

ℹ Atatürk Meydanı ☎ (0232) 633 1862 🕒 summer 8:30–7; winter, Mon–Fri 8:30–12, 12:30–5:30.

↔ Pergamum (➤ 24)

AYVALIK

Ottoman Greeks founded Ayvalık in the 16th century and it was soon the most important town on the coast after İzmir, but after the War of Independence the Greek population was sent to Greece in exchange for Muslims from Lesbos and Crete. The town's mosques are mostly Greek Orthodox churches with minarets added on, and a stroll along cobbled streets from one to another takes you past fine examples of domestic Ottoman architecture. A causeway leads to the island of Alibey, which has fish restaurants, but it is best to go there on one of the boats which regularly depart from the quayside. The dock for boats to and from the Greek island of Lésvos (Lesbos) is close by, a little to the north.

BERGAMA ⭐

Bergama covers part of the glorious ancient city of Pergamum: the lofty acropolis rises at one end of the town, and the Asklepeion lies at the other (➤ 24).

Bergama itself is a workaday market town where a donkey and cart is as likely to run you over as one of the tour buses bringing visitors to Pergamum. The archaeological and enthographic museum is not far from the tourist office, and has a very good collection of statuary from Pergamum. The Kızıl Avlu, the Red Basilica, at the bottom of the acropolis, was originally a pagan temple, but was converted to a basilica by the Byzantines.

BOZCAADA ✪

According to Homer the Greeks hid their fleet at Bozcaada while waiting for the Trojans to take the wooden horse in to Troy (▶ 55). The island is only 5km wide, has no resort hotels and boasts some fine beaches along the south coast. Near where boats dock are the ruins of a vast, originally Byzantine, castle (always open). The traditional architecture in the island's only town has been well preserved, and there are several *pansiyons*.

⊞ 30A5
✉ Just off the coast, south of Troy, 60km southwest of Çanakkale
🍴 Restaurants (£) near quayside
⛴ Ferry from Yükyeri İskelesi (*dolmuş*/minibus from Çanakkale)

ÇANAKKALE ✪✪

Çanakkale lies between East and West, overlooking the narrow Dardanelles strait (▶ 38), with Gallipoli on the far side and Troy just to the south. The place breathes history and mythology, and this romantic atmosphere is enhanced by the coming and going of boats at the docks. It is a pleasant small town in which to pass a lazy day while planning trips to Troy and Gallipoli. Boats also leave for Gökçeada. The docks are the nucleus of the town, and close by are all the hotels and restaurants, and the tourist office. A small bazaar area lies inland between the park and the main dock. A couple of kilometres out of town on the road to Troy, an archaeological museum contains a varied collection of artefacts from the region, including Troy.

⊞ 30A5
✉ 30km northeast of Troy
🍴 Plenty (£–££)
🚌 Buses from Ayvalık, Istanbul, İzmir, Troy
ℹ By dock ☎ (0286) 217 1187
↔ Gallipoli (▶ 44), Troy (▶ 55)
❓ Tours to Gallipoli and Troy

Below: *the seafront in Çanakkale*

ÇANAKKALE BOĞAZI (DARDANELLES) ⭐⭐

The sea lane that connects the Aegean with the Sea of Marmara has had strategic significance for thousands of years, and has played a crucial part in history and mythology. It was seen as the dividing line between Asia and Europe when the Persian army under Xerxes crossed it on the way to invade Greece in 480 BC, and it is still the dividing line today. In 1915 the British and French fleets tried to push through the Dardanelles and capture Istanbul, but failed disastrously (➤ 44). In Greek mythology, a woman called Helle fell into the water while fleeing from her mother-in-law and drowned – hence the strait's ancient name of 'Hellespont' (Helle's sea). In another Greek tale, Leander would swim across to meet his lover, Hero, a priestess of Venus, on the European side. When he was drowned one night, the heartbroken Hero drowned herself too. The poet Byron swam across the Hellespont in 1810.

ÇANDARLI ⭐⭐

This small fishing village emerges from hibernation to become a low-key resort between April and October. Çandarlı, site of ancient Pitane, is a place to relax in, enjoying sea walks along the coarse-sand beach and unhurried meals at one of the seafood restaurants. The atmosphere is laid back but inviting. A well-preserved, 14th-century Genoese castle, not open to the public, lends character to this very pleasant village. The liveliest time to visit is on a Friday, when there is a market.

Çandarlı's popular market is in the town square

Çanakkale to Bursa

This is a long drive and you will need to stay overnight in Bursa. If you want to return to Çanakkale instead, turn back after visiting the Kuşcenneti National Park.

The E90/200 connects Çanakkale with Bursa. The first 45km will take you gently up and down hills to beyond the village of Lipseki (ancient Lampsacus, the traditional birth-place of the phallic god Priapus). There are occasional views of the Dardanelles on the left. Then the road moves inland for about 70km, returning to the coast at Denizkent. Some 35km later, the town of Bandırma is reached.

From Bandırma follow the road to Balıkesir for 13km and look for a sign on the right pointing the 5km-way to the Kuşcenneti National Park (► 49). After visting the park, return to the main road and turn right back onto the E90/200 towards Bandırma. Just under 40km before Bursa, look for a sign pointing right for the fishing village of Gölyazı, 6km from the main road.

Gölyazı is situated by the side of a lake, Uluabat Gölö, and is built over the ruins of ancient Apollonia. Ancient city walls and a large deserted Greek church are the main points of interest besides the pleasant scenes of everyday life in a Turkish fishing village.

Return to the main road and complete the journey to Bursa.

Park your car near the tourist office, in the centre of town, and collect a town map and brochure before setting off to explore the Ottoman houses and other monuments of the city.

Distance
340km
(200km to/from Kuşcenneti National Park)

Time
8–10 hours

Start point
Çanakkale
✚ 30A5

End point
Bursa
✚ 30C5

Lunch
Appolonia Restaurant (£)
✉ North end of the village of Gölyazı

Ottoman architecture in Bursa

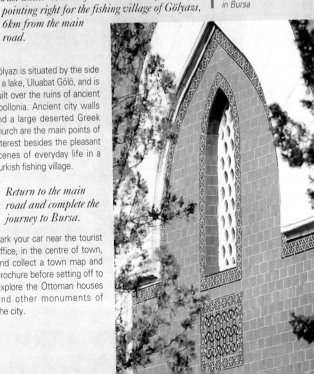

ÇEŞME (► 18, TOP TEN)

CHRYSE ✪

All that remains of Chryse is the ruined temple of Apollo Smintheon, signposted in the village of Gülpınar, but it is a place of significance in Homer's account of the Trojan war. It was from here that the Greek leader Agamemnon took Chryseis, the daughter of the priest of Apollo, for a mistress. He later grudgingly returned her, to appease Apollo, but only after demanding the mistress of Achilles as compensation and causing a major row in the process. This is the place to read Book I of the *Iliad*, and the landscape makes the journey from Assos very pleasant. The road continues west to Babakale, passing a turning on the way to a lovely beach at Akliman.

DİLEK MİLLİ PARKI ✪

This national park covers a large area of mountains, marsh and beaches, but some parts are used by the military and access to these is strictly prohibited. What remains open, however, is amply rewarding for anyone seeking fresh air and a break from ancient temples or busy resorts. From the park's entrance it is about 10km to the last of the pebbly but pretty beaches along the way. The last beach, Karasu, makes a particularly pleasant spot for a picnic. In the higher areas, you should see birds of prey. The marshes have water birds.

EDREMİT AND ÖREN ✪

There is little to interest the tourist in Edremit but visitors travelling by public transport along the north Aegean coast are likely to find themselves waiting for a *dolmuş*/minibus connection here. The village of Burhaniye is about 15km to the south and a *dolmuş*/minibus from here brings one to the pretty low-key resort of Ören, 4km away. There is a splendid beach, and the coastal road heading west towards Küçükukuyu is lined with moderately priced hotels and *pansiyons*.

Sidebar (Chryse):

+ 30A4
⊠ Gülpınar, 20km west of Assos
🍴 Restaurant (£) in Babakale
🚌 Occasional *dolmuş*/minibus from Assos
♿ None
🖐 Free
↔ Assos (► 34)

Sidebar (Dilek Milli Parkı):

+ 30B2
⊠ 30km south of Kuşadası
☎ (0256) 646 1079
🕐 8–6:30
🍴 Snack bars on beaches
🚌 *Dolmuş*/minibus from Kuşadası
♿ None
💷 Cheap
↔ Kuşadası (► 46–7), Priene (► 52)

The Lanner falcon (Falco biarmicus) may be seen in Dilek Milli Parkı

Sidebar (Edremit and Ören):

+ 30B4
⊠ 120km south of Çanakkale
🍴 Local food (£) served in Ören's market; hotel restaurants
🚌 *Dolmuş*/minibus from Çanakkale and Ayvalık
↔ Assos (► 34), Ayvalık (► 36)

Around Efes (Ephesus)

From the ticket office walk straight ahead to the marble-paved path.

The theatre is on the left, and on the right is the Arcadian Way, one of the few streets outside Rome to have street-lighting in ancient times.

Go to the theatre (▶ 19) and climb the steps. You can go straight to the theatre's seating area, or turn right near the top of the steps by the solitary tree, and enter the theatre orchestra through the roofed passageway.
Leave the theatre on the opposite side.

About halfway along the marble-paved street, look for the brothel sign (a footprint and a female face) etched on a pavement stone on the right side, protected by a metal frame.

At the end of this street the two-storey facade of the Celsus Library (▶ 42–3) is on the right. Turn to the left, up a gradually sloping marble-paved street.

On the left a sign indicates an ancient spice shop. Just before it is the entrance to the Roman public toilets; just after the spice shop is Hadrian's Temple. Inside the temple entrance, on the right side, note the 13 carved figures on the walls: Athena with her shield at either end of a group of six Greek deities and five members of Emperor Theodosius' family.

Carry on up the street until a sign points right to the museum of inscriptions.

The delightful odeon (theatre) up on the left makes an ideal picnic stop. You can leave from the Upper Entrance, just ahead, or retrace your route to the Lower Entrance.

Distance
2km (4km if returning to start point)

Time
3–4 hours

Start Point
Lower Entrance
✚ 30B3

End Point
Upper Entrance/Lower Entrance
✚ 30B3

Lunch
The restaurants at the Lower Entrance are not recommended. Bring a picnic and, on a hot day, a lot of drinks

This temple at Ephesus is dedicated to the Emperor Hadrian

🔲 30B3
✉ 3km from Selçuk tourist office
☎ (0232) 892 6402/6940
🕐 Summer 8–6:30; winter 8–5:30
🍴 Restaurants (not recommended) at the Lower Entrance. Bring a picnic or eat in Selçuk (£–££)
🚌 Buses to Selçuk from Kuşadası and İzmir

EFES (EPHESUS) ✪✪✪

Ephesus was the capital of the Roman province of Asia Minor. It was a major political and cultural centre, and the Romans spared no expense in making this a showcase city for their civilisation. It has been very well preserved and is one of the major ancient sites around the Mediterranean. Long before the Romans, Ephesus was home to the cult of Cybele, a mother-goddess. Cybele merged easily with the Greek goddess Artemis, worshipped by the Athenian colonisers who founded a settlement here around 1000 BC. Ephesus flourished under Rome and was abandoned only in the sixth century AD after the harbour had silted up.

At least half a day is needed to explore the city (see the Efes walk, ➤ 41). You can join a guided tour but a guide is not essential because the site is compact and there are many specialist guidebooks at the entrance, in the Selçuk tourist office or in the bookshop across the road from it. Visitors may be irritated by the number of areas that are off-limits. This is mainly due to prolonged restoration work by an Austrian archaeological project, which makes Ephesus look like a construction site, complete with massive cranes. The highlights include the theatre (➤ 19) and the Library of Celsus. The

> ### Did you know ?
>
> *When Mark Twain visited Ephesus he found 'exquisitely sculptured marble fragments scattered thick among the dust and weeds' (The Innocents Abroad, 1869). H V Morton made a visit in 1936, and noted 'no sign of life but a goat herd leaning on a broken sarcophagus or a lonely peasant outlined against a mournful sunset. Few people ever visit it.' This is a far cry from the scene today but, out of season, it is still possible to wander through the city virtually alone.*

scant remains of the temple of Artemis, one of the Seven Wonders of the Ancient World, are passed on the walk from Selçuk to the entrance (signposted as the Artemision, on the left side of the road).

The Library of Celsus, built between AD 110 and 135, is an impressive and beautiful structure. The four niches on the two-storeyed façade are filled with plaster copies of the statues of the Four Virtues – Goodness, Thought, Knowledge and Wisdom – whose originals now reside in Vienna. Beyond the three-arched gateway on the north (right) side is the main agora (market place – it may be off-limits). Graffiti, both ancient and modern, adorns the walls of the gateway. One inscription in Greek praises the work of a food inspector in fixing the price of bread sold in the agora. The library could hold some 14,000 book scrolls. Peer through the grill in the front right corner to see the metre-wide cavity that protected them from winter damp.

The marbled street that runs uphill from the Library of Celsus (► 41) has been completely restored, showing the toilets, baths, shops, homes and a temple as they once were. At the top of this street, one relief is all that remains of the Gate of Hercules. Here the way branches to the right for the temple to Domitian, one of Rome's madder emperors (AD 81–96). The left branch leads past a temple, and on to an odeon, a 1,400-seat theatre, which has been restored.

🛈 In Selçuk ☎ (0232) 892 1328

♿ None

🍴 Moderate

↔ Selçuk (► 53), Meryemana (► 50), Kuşadası (► 46–7), Magnesia on the Maeander (► 49)

❓ Regular tours from most resorts

Below: *looking up at the meticulously restored façade of the Library of Celsus (bottom)*

🚩 30A3
✉ 70km northwest of İzmir
🍴 Restaurants (£–££)
ℹ Just north of central
square ☎ (0232) 812
1222
🚌 Bus from İzmir
↔ Çandarlı (➤ 38), İzmir
(➤ 31)

🚩 30A5
✉ 35km-long peninsula
opposite Çanakkale
🕐 Sites are open 24 hours;
🍴 Restaurants (£–££) in
Gelibolu
🚢 Passenger and vehicle
ferry from Çanakkale, or
join a tour
♿ None
↔ Çanakkale (➤ 37), Troy
(➤ 55)
❓ Tours available

Military Museum
☎ (0283) 814 1297
💷 Cheap
🕐 8:30–5:30, closed 12–1 in
winter

FOÇA

Nowadays a summer haunt of İzmir's well-to-do, the town was founded in ancient times by Greek colonists who called it Phocaea. The Phoceans were famed seafarers, and are credited with founding Massilia (Marseilles). Apart from a 4th-century BC tomb, Taş Kule, there is precious little left of the ancient city, but it is a pretty place with some fish restaurants. A restored Genoese fortress lies 8km east of town on the main road.

GELİBOLU (GALLIPOLI) ⭐⭐

Gelibolu, a nondescript town on the narrow peninsula of land opposite Çanakkale Boğazıçı (Dardanelles), is synonymous with a momentous battle of World War I. When the French and British fleets failed to force their way through the Dardanelles (➤ 38), Winston Churchill ordered a troop landing in order to knock out the Turkish troops guarding the strait. The aim was to secure the Dardanelles, take İstanbul, and organise logistical support for their Russian allies through the Black Sea, but the plan failed in the face of furious Turkish resistance. Thousands of Allied soldiers were killed and over 55,000 Turks lost their lives. There are organised tours of the battlefield sites and memorials from Çanakkale.

AnaTur tour, with Ali Efe ☎ (0286) 217 5482, whose grandfather died at Gallipoli, is recommended. Also based in Çanakkale, Down Under Agency ☎ (0286) 217 3343 runs tours lasting most of a day. They usually include, a viewing of an Australian documentary on the campaign, and the movie *Gallipoli* with Mel Gibson the night before. You will need your own transport if you do not join an organised tour, because the sites are spread out across a wide area.

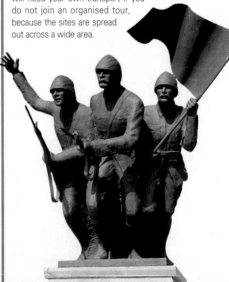

*The war memorial
on the Gelibolu
(Gallipoli) peninsula*

GÖKÇEADA ✪

The larger of Turkey's two islands close to Çanakkale Boğazıçı (Dardanelles), in the North Aegean (the other is Bozcaada, ➤ 37), Gökçeada has the open prison from which William Hayes, of *Midnight Express* fame, escaped. You will need your own transport to reach the island's small villages. There is a pleasant beach on the north coast at Kaleköy, which can also be reached by *dolmuş*.

HERAKLEIA ✪✪✪

Originally part of the ancient kingdom of Caria, Herakleia was fortified and Hellenised in the 4th century BC. The signposted sites are spread out, around and in the small village of Kapıkırı. A good place to start is at the sanctuary of Endymion (see below). As you walk towards the road from the sanctuary, a sign points to Carian rock tombs on the right. To see them, clamber over the wall and head for the remains of a Byzantine castle on the headland. From the rocks on the other side of the castle walls you can look down on the Carian coffins cut out of the rock.

HIERAPOLIS (➤ 20, TOP TEN)

🚩	30A5
⊠	30km west of Çanakkale
🍴	Fish restaurants (£)
🚢	Ferry from Çanakkale
🔄	Çanakkale (➤ 37), Troy (➤ 55), Çanakkale Boğazıçı(➤ 38), Gallipoli(➤ 44)

🚩	30B2
⊠	In village of Kapıkırı
🕐	Open access at all times
🍴	Restaurants (£)
🚌	*Dolmuş*/minibus from Çamiçi or by boat across Lake Bafa
♿	None
💷	Free
🔄	Euromos (➤ 68), Labranda (➤ 77), Milas (➤ 83), Drive from Kuşadası (➤ 48)

Did you know ?

According to tradition, Zeus granted Endymion his wish for eternal youth by sending him to sleep and dream for ever on Mount Latmos. The moon goddess, Selene, fell in love with him and bore him fifty daughters while he slept.

Above: *The modern village of Kapıkırı has developed next to the ruins of ancient Herakleia*

45

KUŞADASI ⚫⚫

This is one of the major resorts on the Aegean coast and unashamedly proclaimed as such by the scores of carpet shops, jewellers and leatherware stores that fill the town centre. The large harbour, which in summer receives half a dozen cruise ships each day, faces Samos, and the 2km trip to the Greek island is a popular diversion for people staying in Kuşadası. Kuşadası offers a wide range of entertainment in addition to shopping. At night the pubs, discos (▶ 112–13), Turkish baths (▶ 115) and restaurants (▶ 94–5) are bursting at the seams with happy holidaymakers determined to have a good time. During the day, water-based activities are very popular, and most of the big hotels are able to offer a wide range of sports.

Kuşadası is so dedicated to hedonism that the lack of places of interest within the town itself hardly matters; the most interesting site is the small Bird Island, connected to the mainland by a 400m causeway and home to a 16th-century Genoese fortress, which has been converted into discos and cafés. Kuşadası is well placed, however, for visits to many of the Turkish Aegean's most extraordinary ancient sites. Ephesus is a short bus ride away, and the ancient Greek settlements of Milet (Miletus), Didim (Didyma) and Priene may be easily visited on public transport or on a three-in-a-day guided tour. Aphrodisias, Pamukkale and Hierapolis are a couple of hours away by road.

The main esplanade, Atatürk Bulvarı, runs past the harbour where boats to and from Samos dock. The nearby Öküz Mehmet Pasa

The Genoese castle on Bird Island bustles with cafés and discos

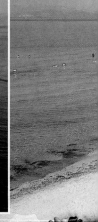

Kervansaray (now a noisy hotel) is a useful landmark in this town, which has no obvious centre. At the junction of the hotel and the esplanade, a pedestrianised street, Barbaros Hayrettin Bulvarı, runs inland. To the left, as you ascend this street, lies the old part of town, known as Kale, where some picturesque buildings have been converted into discos, bars and restaurants.

Kadinlar Plaji (Ladies' Beach), 3km southwest of town and easily reached by minibus, has a cluster of resort hotels and is very well known, but the cleaner pools of nearby hotels may seem more inviting. A better choice is Tusan beach, 5km from the other side of town out on the road to Selçuk and also easily reached by minibus.

Moderately priced accommodation is available near the town centre; the 4- and 5-star hotels are stretched out in bunches along the coastline either end of town, but they are nearly all easily reached by minibuses from the seafront road. These minibuses will usually stop opposite the main bus station, which is outside town on the main İzmir–Söke road. This can be an uncomfortably long walk in summer, but to get to Söke (the major local transport hub and the departure point for buses to places of historical interest) there is an unofficial minibus meeting point nearer to the centre of town, and most of the hotel minibuses also stop here.

Ladies' Beach welcomes both sexes throughout the year

Ancient Caria

Distance
178km

Time
4–6 hours, depending of length of stops

Start/end point
Kuşadası
✚ 30B3

Lunch
Zeybek or Agora restaurant (£)

This drive leaves from the hustle and bustle of Kuşadası to explore the ancient kingdom of Caria, taking in Lake Bafa and a number of interesting Hellenic sites, some of which are difficult to reach without your own transport.

From Kuşadası take the road to Söke (515) and when it meets the main İzmir–Milas road, the 525, turn right, signposted for Milas, and head south. Once the road starts to hug the shores of Lake Bafa park by one of the lake-side restaurants.

It is possible to take a swim in the lake, and there are passenger boats to Herakleia (➤ 45). This drive, however, will reach Herakleia by road.

Bafa Gölü (Lake Bafa) with ancient Herakleia on the far side

Drive on about 6km to the village of Çamiçi and take the road signposted left to Herakleia. After visiting Herakleia, return to Çamiçi and turn right to continue towards Milas for about 15km. Look for a signpost on the left to Euromos (➤ 68), just 1km south of the village of Selimiye.

After visiting Euromos, continue for another 12km and turn left at the sign for Kargıcak if you wish to make the 14km detour to Labranda (➤ 77). If the road surfacing has not been completed, only the first few kilometres will be paved and some driving in low gears will be necessary.

Return to the main road. If time permits, it is only a few kilometres further on to Milas (➤ 83). Otherwise, turn right when meeting the main road from Kargıcak and return to Kuşadası.

KUŞCENNETİ MİLLİ PARKI ⭐

This bird sanctuary, whose name translates as 'Bird Paradise', lies between Çanakkale and Bursa (➤ 39). An exhibit inside the entrance shows what birds may be seen from the nearby observation post (bring your own binoculars). Herons, cormorants, pelicans and spoonbills frequent the reserve and you may see the occasional spotted eagle. Between April and June, and from September to November are the best times to visit because so many species migrate at these times. Over 250 species have been identified.

➕ 30B5
✉ 20km south of Bandırma
🕐 7–5:30
🚌 Bus from Çanakkale
♿ None
💰 Cheap

Spoonbills (Platalea leucorodia) grace Kuşcenneti National Park with their presence

LAODIKEIÁ (LAODICEIA) ⭐

Ancient Laodiceia was founded in the 3rd century BC and flourished until an earthquake in the 5th century AD. The city inspired St John the Divine's acerbic comment on a civilian population that failed to embrace Christianity as quickly as he anticipated: 'I know your works, you are neither hot nor cold... So because you are lukewarm, and neither hot nor cold, I will spew you out of my mouth.' The Roman ruins include a gymnasium and baths, two theatres and the remnants of a stadium. There is no public transport to the site; you can get a taxi in Pamukkale but it is best to drive yourself.

➕ 30C3
✉ 14km south of Pamukkale, 5km north of Denizli
🕐 Open 24 hours
🚌 Taxi from Pamukkale
♿ None
💰 Free
🔁 Pamukkale (➤ 22–3), Hierapolis (➤ 20), Aphrodisias (➤ 34)

MAGNESIA ON THE MAEANDER ⭐

Homesick colonists from Magnesia in Greece founded this ancient city and it was presented to the Athenian Themistocles by a Persian king. He is said to have committed suicide here while making a sacrifice at the Temple of Artemis. It requires some imagination to make sense of the scattered remains of this temple but you are likely to have the place to yourself, which gives it a certain charm.

➕ 30B3
✉ 16km north of Söke
🕐 8:30–dusk
🚌 Dolmuş/minibus from Söke or Selçuk
💰 Cheap
🔁 Ephesus (➤ 42–3), Meryemana (➤ 50), Kuşadası (➤ 46–7)

MANİSA ✪

Founded in the aftermath of the fall of Troy and destroyed by Greeks soldiers retreating in 1922 (➤ 10–11), contemporary Manisa is a modern town with a commercial air, redeemed by a grand backdrop of mountains and a city centre worth a half day's exploration. The tourist office is in the centre of town and you can pick up a map and brochure there before setting out to visit the town's three 16th-century mosques and a small museum with material from Sart (Sardis) (➤ 53).

MERYEMANA ✪

The story that the Virgin Mary came to Ephesus with St Paul gained credibility in the early 19th century, when a German nun who had never been to Turkey described a vision of the house where Mary stayed. A priest in İzmir matched the description with a chapel just south of Ephesus. Sanctioned by a papal visit in 1967, Meryemana is now regarded as the place where Mary lived out her last years, and receives a steady stream of pilgrims.

MİLET (MILETOS) ✪

By far the most important of the Greek colonies established along the Aegean coast, Miletos was originally on an inlet of the sea, but a marshy delta has now formed around the site. The remains you see today belong to the city re-created after a destructive onslaught by the Persians in 495 BC. When a play on the Persian defeat of

Miletos was performed in ancient Athens the audience burst into tears and the playwright was fined for causing such dismay. The large theatre is a good vantage point from which to view the site, which was laid out in a grid pattern (still visible). Parts of a nymphaeum (fountain), *agora* (market place), and Roman baths survive.

NOTİON AND KLAROS ✪

Notion was a typically small ancient Greek settlement, and although very little remains today the site is attractively located and offers a fine view of the sea. Signposts lead from Notion to the site of ancient Klaros just over 1km away. Never a city, Klaros was famed for its temple and oracle of Apollo (presently undergoing excavation and restoration), whose priest was able to answer the needs of those making a consultation without ever hearing their question. The source of inspiration was a sacred spring and parts of the underground chamber enclosing it can be clearly made out.

NYSSA ✪

Many of Turkey's minor ancient Greek and Roman sites have attractive settings, and Nyssa's is especially so. The city was founded in the 3rd century BC and flourished well into Roman times. Strabo, a geographer of the first century BC, described it as a 'double city' and there are some remains of two bridges that linked the settlement across a tumultuous stream. A well-preserved theatre and a semi-circular bouleuterion (meeting hall) are the main sights; the long tunnel that the citizens built to help drain the city can also be made out. Nyssa is not visited by tour buses but it is easy to reach by car or public transport and, like Notion and Klaros (► above), makes a good day trip from Kuşadası.

PAMUKKALE (► 21–22, TOP TEN)

PERGAMUM (► 24, TOP TEN)

Seats in the theatre of Miletos, and a detail from a fallen column

🚌 *Dolmuş*/minibus from Söke
♿ None
🍴 Cheap
↔ Priene (► 52), Didyma (► 66)
❓ Tours from Kuşadası combine Miletos, Priene and Didyma

➕ 30B3
✉ 25km north of Kuşadası
🕐 Dawn–dusk
🚌 *Dolmuş*/minibus from Kuşadası to Seferihisar. Ask for Notion
♿ None
🎟 Free
↔ Kuşadası (► 46–7), Ephesus (► 41–3), Selçuk (► 53)

➕ 30B3
✉ 2km from Sultanhisar, 14km west of Nazilli
🕐 8:30–dusk
🍴 Restaurants (£) in Sultanhisar
🚌 Buses between Kuşadası and Denizli will stop at Sultanhisar
♿ None
🎟 Cheap
↔ Aydın (► 35)

+ 30B2
⊠ 35km south of Kuşadası
☎ (0256) 547 1165
⏰ 8:30–sunset
🍴 Restaurants (£) in
adjoining village of
Güllübahçe
🚌 Dolmuş/minibus from
Söke
♿ None
💰 Cheap
🔄 Kuşadası (► 46–7),
Ephesus (► 19 and
41–3), Selçuk (► 53),
Meryemana (► 50),
Miletos (► 50), Didyma
(► 66), Magnesia on the
Maeander (► 49)
❓ Tours from Kuşadası
combine Priene, Miletos
and Didyma

*Above: the ancient city of
Priene makes an
enjoyable day's excursion
from Kuşadası*

52

PRIENE ★★★

Ancient Priene, founded around the 11th century BC, now
lies under the alluvial plain, but the city that developed
from the 4th century BC is remarkably well preserved. It
never attracted much attention from the Romans, and the
happy result for today's visitor is a Hellenistic city unclut-
tered by Roman or Byzantine additions and modifications.
The theatre should not be missed: the front row has five
marble thrones for special guests, and faces the altar of
Dionysus, where a sacrifice began the day's entertainment. The two-storey stage structure and its projecting
proscenium have, to a remarkable degree, weathered the
last 2,000 years, and the holes and sockets for decorated
wooden panels may be clearly seen on some of the front
pillars which held up the stage.

The Temple of Athena Polias is the most dramatic of
the remains and some of the columns have been re-
erected. In ancient times, it was regarded as the epitome
of Ionic temple architecture. When English archaeologists
arrived in the 1860s the temple walls were still standing
over 1.5m in places. To the north of the temple lie the
scant remains of a sanctuary to Demeter and Kore; far
more substantial are the remains of the bouleuterion
(meeting hall) to the south of the theatre. The gymnasium
and small stadium, on the south, lower front side of the
site, are worth seeking out. Some of the starting blocks for
foot races can still be made out.

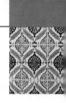

SART (SARDIS) ✪✪

There are two main sites: the Greek Temple of Artemis and the Roman city of the 5th century AD. The wonderful Temple of Artemis is signposted on the right, as you come from İzmir, and is reached after a 1km walk. The setting is idyllic: it is surrounded by pinnacles of rock, with the occasional tinkling of sheep bells in the background as a shepherd moves his flock. Although only two columns remain completely upright, there is plenty to inspire the imagination. An Ionic capital, resting in front of a rusting crane left behind by excavators, is reputed to be one of the best examples you are likely to see at such close quarters. The Roman town has been excavated and restored.

SELÇUK ✪✪

The tourist industry in this small town is entirely due to its proximity to Ephesus. It makes an ideal place for a short stay because it is also close to the ancient sites south of Kuşadası. The Ephesus Museum displays finds from Ephesus: do not miss the Artemis room, with its many-breasted statue of the goddess. The adjoining ethnographic section is also recommended. The Hill of Ayasoluk towers over the town, with Byzantine-Turkish fortifications and the remains of St John's Basilica, built to mark the final resting place of St John the Evangelist. From Selçuk you can make a pleasant day trip to the old Greek town of Sirince, only 8km away.

✚ 30B3
✉ 100km east of İzmir
🕐 8–6
🍴 Restaurant (£) opposite Roman ruins or go to Salihli (9km)
🚌 Bus from İzmir
♿ None
💰 Cheap

A visit to the Ephesus Museum in Selçuk complements a day among the ruins

✚ 30B3
✉ 20km northeast of Kuşadası
🍴 Restaurants (£–££)
🚌 Bus from İzmir, *dolmuş*/minibus from Ephesus, Kuşadası
ℹ Atatürk Mah ☎ (0232) 892 6328 🕐 8:30–5:30 (7PM in high season)
↔ Kuşadası (➤ 46–7), Ephesus (➤ 19 and 41–3)

53

✚ 30A3
✉ 40km southwest of İzmir
🕐 Open 24 hours
🍴 Restaurants (£) in Sığacık
🚌 *Dolmuş*/minibus from İzmir
♿ None
💲 Free
↔ İzmir (► 31), Çeşme (► 18)

A tiny harbour and the remains of a Genoese fortress dominate the fishing village of Sığacık

SİĞACIK AND TEOS

The lack of a sandy beach ensures that Sığacık, a village that has grown up inside the walls of a Genoese fortress, remains a low-key destination. Just 1.5km away the beach at Akkum is a developing resort that may in time affect the character of Sığacık. The site of ancient Teos, 5km from Sığacık, is the best reason for visiting this stretch of coastline between İzmir and Çeşme. Freya Stark wrote: 'It is where I should live, if I had the choice of all the cities of Ionia.' The city was the birthplace of the lyric poet Anakreon (*c* 540 BC) and was a renowned centre for the cult of Dionysus, a Greek nature god of vegetation and fruitfulness, particularly associated with wine and ecstasy. The remains of a Temple of Dionysus, once the largest in the ancient world, are the ruined site's main attraction.

TRUVA (TROY) ✪✪

Troy was thought to have existed only in Homer's imagination until excavations began in 1870, financed by the German businessman Heinrich Schliemann, who was obsessed with finding the historical city. He discovered not one but four settlements, built over the ruins of each other, and later excavations suggest that there were nine main periods of occupation. The first five, known as Troy 1 to Troy V (3000 BC–1800 BC), follow a similar cultural pattern, but a change then occurs, as prosperity grew from maritime trading links in the Aegean and the Black Sea. This could have brought conflict with the Greeks, who besiege Troy in Homer's *Iliad*. The epic poem tells a highly charged tale of war, love and honour, aided and hindered by the pantheon of Greek gods. It was enormously influential not only for the ancient Greeks, but for later European civilisation itself.

Homer's Troy may have been Troy VI (1800–1275 BC), which was destroyed by an earthquake in 1275 BC or by being stormed and set on fire (or both, over time). Settlements of the site went on into Roman times, with Troy IX (300 BC–AD 300) completing the saga. The enormous wooden horse at the entrance to Troy leaves no doubt as to which of the city's many eras captures the interest of modern visitors.

There is a lot to see, but it is a place of ditches, mounds and fragments rather than great structures. The whole site is surprisingly small, or perhaps only the crowds make it seem so; it is worth turning up early in the morning or as late as possible. When viewed from the city walls, the dismally flat plain that stretches ahead can be evocative of ancient battles and, with only a little imagination, the 300m-stretch of inward-leaning and curving wall of Troy VI will conjure up images of the scene of Hector being dragged by furious Achilles around the city walls. Inside the city one of the most impressive sights is the massive stone ramp that could have carried the Wooden Horse – except that it belongs to Troy II (2500–2300 BC).

➕ 30A5
✉ 25km south of Çanakkale
☎ (0286) 283 0061
🕐 8:30–sunset
🚌 *Dolmuş*/minibus from Çanakkale
♿ None
💲 Cheap
↔ Çanakkale (➤ 37), Çanakkale Boğaziçi (➤ 38), Gallipoli (➤ 44)
❓ Tours from Çanakkale often include Gallipoli (➤ 37)

A wooden horse at Troy

Did you know ?

The Trojan treasures that Schliemann took back to Berlin were lost without trace after the Russians took the city in May 1945. They reappeared at an exhibition in Moscow in 1993.

Southern Aegean

Turkey's southern Aegean coast has experienced tourism on a large scale for far longer than the north. Nevertheless, the chief resort town of Bodrum has retained a surprising charm, and it remains one of the most pleasant destinations along the self-styled Turkish Riviera. Its competitor Marmaris is just a little further south; the ease of visiting the Greek island of Ródos (Rhodes) from here is a major attraction. At Marmaris the coast begins to turn westwards, and is known as the Turquoise Coast because of the opaque sky-blue and green-blue colours of the Mediterranean. The small town of Fethiye is an attractive base for a sun, sea and sand holiday but it is also in easy reach of several fascinating historical sites, dating back to the ancient kingdom of Lycia that once included this corner of the coast.

> '*The life loving and prosperous people of Physcus [ancient Marmaris] are blessed with the world's most beautiful rainbow by day, and at night, a moon that hangs over the sea like a ball of fire.*'
>
> HERODOTUS, *The Histories*
> 5th century BC

Open-air restaurants beneath Bodrum Castle

ⓘ Barış Meydanı 48
☎ (0252) 316 1091
⊙ Summer 8:30–7;
winter Mon–Fri
8:30–noon, 1–5:30
🚌 Buses from Fethiye,
İzmir, Kuşadası,
Marmaris, Pamukkale
↔ Milas (➤ 83), Turgutreis
(➤ 89)

Bodrum

Contemporary Bodrum is a major resort, but still has a traditional Mediterranean flavour, with whitewashed, flat-roofed homes dotting the terraced hillsides. The recent opening of an international airport has given a fresh boost to its thriving tourist industry, and despite lacking its own beach, Bodrum is the most chic and European resort on Turkey's Aegean coast.

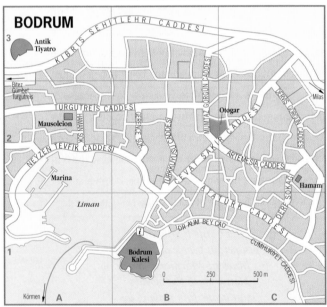

The original name of the town was Halicarnassus and it was founded in the 11th century BC by Greek colonists. Notable inhabitants have included the historian Herodotus (5th century BC), and Mausolus (377–353 BC), who was installed as King after a Persian invasion. Halicarnassus fell into obscurity during Roman and Byzantine times, until the Knights of St John arrived from nearby Rhodes in 1402 and built the massive castle that continues to tower over the town. The word *bodrum* means 'dungeon' or 'underground vault' in Turkish, and the town's modern name presumably derives from either the castle or the Mausoleum.

The Castle of St Peter is the obvious landmark and directly in front of it, due north, is the tourist office. The pedestrianised streets to the north of the tourist office make up the town's bazaar and this is the central shopping area for leather, clothes, carpets and assorted souvenirs and gifts. Dr Alim Bey Caddesi is the main street facing the sea to the east. At the end of the bazaar area the street becomes Cumhuriyet Caddesi, and forms the heart of Bodrum's legendary nightlife. The sea-facing street that follows the harbour's curve to the west of the tourist office, Nezen Tevfik Caddesi, brings you past open-air restaurants and cafés to the marina and the quieter end of town. The main street into the centre from the bus station, Cevat İşakir Caddesi, has more shops, restaurants, and the post office.

During the high season Bodrum is definitely not a place for anyone seeking a quiet retreat; the sophisticated discos are the loudest on the coast. The mornings in Bodrum are relatively quiet, but only because so many visitors are sound asleep after carousing and dancing till dawn. The beaches that dot Bodrum's peninsula (➤ 62) are fast developing into resorts in their own right.

Bodrum's marina is a favourite destination for yachts plying the Aegean and Mediterranean, and the town is an ideal place to organise a sailing excursion. Yachts and boats can be hired with or without a crew, and there is no problem finding an agent who will arrange a day trip for those with no experience of sailing. Excursions off the peninsula by road, on the other hand, begin with an hour-long drive to the main coast road. If you are touring, a two-night stay should be sufficient, although the peninsula has plenty to offer by way of sandy beaches, accommodation and restaurants for a lazy couple of weeks.

The medieval Castle of St Peter stands guard over modern Bodrum

Bodrum

Distance
5km

Time

Walk from the tourist office with the water on your left until you reach a Y-junction after a few hundred metres. Bear right, passing the minaret of a mosque on the right, and walk up Cevat Sakir Caddesi.

There is an interesting antique shop on the right, opposite the post office. Turn right into Atatürk Caddesi. This street is filled with signs for small shops, *pansiyons* and cafés.

After about 500m look for a cluster of blue signs for a Turkish bath (hamam), *and the Zozo, Anfora and Sengül pansiyons, all pointing to the left. Turn left here. Shortly after passing the* hamam, *turn left into Artemisia Caddesi and continue to the end of this road. Back on Cevat Sakir Caddesi, turn left.*

For general tourist shopping Bodrum has a good variety of merchandise

There is a fruit market on the right. The row of souvenir shops opposite, includes an interesting jewellery shop.

Just past this shop, cross the road and turn right down Eski Hükümet Sokak, a lane leading to Türkkuyusu Caddesi. Turn right for a good place for lunch. Continue up the road to the T-junction and turn left.

The Picante restaurant is on the right. The Mausoleum (➤ 61) is just over 500m along this road.

Turn right from the Mausoleum and take the first right, which leads down to the harbour close to the marina.

What to See in Bodrum

BEACHES ✪

The nearest beach on the Bodrum Peninsula itself is Gümbet, 3km away and easily reached by *dolmuş*, or on foot when the temperature drops – take the road inland after passing the marina. Gümbet, overdeveloped with package hotels, is the preserve of 18–30-year-olds. Further west there is a mediocre beach at the more upmarket Bitez, and a better one at Ortakent (which is popular with Turkish families on holiday).

Kagı, Bağla, Karaincir and Akyarlar, on the south coast of the peninsula, are quieter locations but still have water sports (equipment is available for hire), and cleaner sea than the beaches nearer Bodrum.

➕ 30B2
🍴 Restaurants and beach cafés (£–££)
🚍 *Dolmuş*/minibus/boat from Bodrum
↔ Turgutreis (➤ 89), Gümbet (➤ 72), Yalıkavak (➤ 90)

> ## *Did you know ?*
>
> *Bodrum has a reputation as the capital of cosmopolitan nightlife on the Aegean coast. The spectacular open-air Disco Halikarnas on Cumhuriyet Caddesi (➤ 114), accommodates over 2,000 stomping dancers until the sun begins to rise over the harbour, and there are scores of smaller but equally lively discos and bars.*

BODRUM KALESI (CASTLE OF ST PETER ➤ 17, TOP TEN)

GÖKOVA KÖRFEZI (GULF OF GÖKOVA) ✪✪

There are boats, yachts and agents for day trips along Dr Alim Bey Caddesi near the tourist office, and at the main marina, off Neyzen Tevfik Caddesi. The typical itinerary visits the island of Karaada, which has hot springs and mud baths, before continuing to Ortakent beach (➤ 84), and skirting the Greek island of Kos, for a swim and lunch. Boats returning to Bodrum often pause at a shallow stretch of water christened the Aquarium because of the marine life that can be seen.

➕ 30B2
❓ See also separate entry for Gökova Korfesi (➤ 72)

Snorkelling is one of the most enjoyable and easy-to-organise watersports along the Aegean coast

🟥 59A2
✉ Turgutreis Caddesi
🕐 Daily 8–5
🍴 None near
♿ None
💷 Cheap

*Above: jet skis can be
hired from the beaches
around Bodrum*

🟥 59A3
🚌 *Dolmuş*/minibus

MAUSOLEION (MAUSOLEUM)

Mausolus ruled ancient Caria for the Persians as a semi-independent state and his love of Greek culture reached its zenith in the splendid tomb – the first 'mausoleum' – erected after his death in 351 BC. It was one of the Seven Wonders of the Ancient World, but the Knights of St John demolished it to get materials for their castle. The massive foundations remain, but little else – assorted column pieces, parts of the outer wall and underground vault. The site is still worth a visit, as an informative exhibition with models gives some flesh to the meagre remains. There are also plaster copies, plus a few original pieces, of the so-called Amazon reliefs that were mostly shipped off to join other hijacked treasures in the British Museum.

TIYATRO (THEATRE) ⭐

To the northwest of the mausoleum, the ancient theatre has been completely restored. It was started by Mausolus, extensively adapted by the Romans, and is now used to hold events during the town's autumn festival. The view is somewhat marred by the noise from the main road.

*Plenty of empty seats at
Bodrum's ancient theatre*

From Bodrum

Catch the morning car ferry from Bodrum to Körmen. The tourist office has ferry departure times. From here it is a 10-minute drive across the peninsula to the town of Datça (▶ 65).

Distance
185km

Time
3–5 hours

Start/end Point
Bodrum
✚ 59B1

Lunch
Plenty of choice in town
(£–££)

On the way to Datça, a signposted road on the right leads west to Knidos (▶ 76) at the end of the peninsula. The road is not a good one, however, so unless you cannot wait to get there by boat, carry straight on here, for Datça.

Turn left to take the main road (400) to Marmaris (about one hour).

Marmaris (▶ 80–1) is the best place to stop for lunch.

From Marmaris, follow the signs to Muğla.

Beehives are dotted about in the surrounding forest: this is where the renowned pine-scented honey of Marmaris comes from.

About 12km after passing a right turn to Fethiye, turn right off the main road, following the signpost to Muğla.

Collecting the famous Marmaris honey

Alexander the Great marched his army through this mountain pass but your vehicle will make the journey in far less time. There are fine views of the Gulf of Gökova, with space to park and take in the scenery.

From Muğla (▶ 83), follow signs to Yatağan, which will bring you back to the main road. At Yatağan turn left for Milas (▶ 83) and from there turn south for Bodrum.

Below: *The beach at Calis suggests itself as a quiet alternative to the ever-busy Ölüdeniz*

What to see in the Southern Aegean

ALTINKUM ✪

'Lazy by day, lively by night' is one travel brochure's catch-phrase for this popular package holiday destination. The splendid 1km-long beach is deservedly popular, especially with British visitors, and is invaded daily by residents of the numerous hotels and *pansiyons* lined up behind the beach. There are tourist restaurants and a modern shopping centre specialising in goods such as watches and designer-label clothes. Of more enduring value, the superb temple of Apollo at Didyma (➤ 66) is just five minutes' drive up the road.

BOZBURUN ✪

This is not a typical Turkish Aegean seaside village. There is a harbour but no beach. It has a range of accommodation, and a number of good restaurants patronised by well-off city families. Boats stop here for lunch, and there is good swimming from the rocks.

CALIS ✪

This is the nearest beach, albeit a shingle one, to Fethiye and the two places are linked by regular public transport on road and sea. The beach is some 2km in length, and runs parallel to the road, which is closed to traffic in the high season. There is the usual array of hotels, bars and restaurants but, on the whole, Calis is a lot quieter and more pleasant than nearby Hisarönü.

✚ 30B2
✉ 5km south of Didyma
🍴 Tourist restaurants (£–££)
🚌 *Dolmuş*/minibus from Kuşadası
↔ Didyma (➤ 66)

✚ 30B1
✉ 30km west of Marmaris
🍴 Quayside restaurants (£–££)
🚌 *Dolmuş*/minibus from Marmaris

✚ 30C1
✉ 5km north of Fethiye
🍴 Restaurants (£–££)
🚌 *Dolmuş*/minibus or ferry *dolmuş* from Fethiye
↔ Fethiye (➤ 68–9), Hisarönü (➤ 73)

Above and left: *enjoying good healthy mud at Dalyan*

DALYAN ✪✪

Dalyan is close to an airport and the main coast road, with Marmaris to the west and the sites of ancient Lycia to the east. Boats leave the quayside every day before 10AM to make the 40-minute journey to İztuzu beach, which is excellent for swimming as well as being a nesting site of the loggerhead turtle between May and October. Development has been prohibited here because the young turtles seem to be confused by bright lights. You can spend a day at İztuzu and return at half-hourly intervals in the afternoon. The beach has little shade, so take hats and suncream. Another popular excursion is a ten-minute boat ride upriver to thermal baths at Ilıca. A wallow in the open-air mud pools, which reach a temperature of 40°C, is said to do the body a power of good. In cooler months it is pleasant to hire a bicycle in Dalyan and cycle to the ancient ruins at Kaunos (➤ 75).

🕂 30C2
✉ 13km south of the main Muğla–Fethiye road
🍴 Restaurants (£–££)
🚌 *Dolmuş*/minibus to Marmaris, Muğla and Fethiye
🔄 Kaunos (➤ 75), Köyceğiz (➤ 76)
❓ Day tours from Dalyan combine İztuzu beach, Kaunos and Köyceğiz

DATÇA ✪

This town, centrally located along the long and narrow peninsula that stretches west from Marmaris, has most of its shops and facilities laid out along one long main street. Its harbour is attracting a growing number of yachts, and the town is slowly developing services for tourists: hotels, restaurants and bars with music are dotted along the seafront. Boat trips go to ancient Knidos and to various swimming places away from the town itself. The best place for swimming close to town is at the far side of the west beach.

🕂 30B2
✉ 75km west of Marmaris
ℹ In centre ☎ (0252) 712 3163
🍴 Restaurants (£–££)
🚌 *Dolmuş*/minibus from Marmaris and Muğla, car ferry from Körmen, 9km north, to Bodrum (➤ 63)
🔄 Knidos (➤ 76), Marmaris (➤ 80–1)

65

Medusa, despite the serpents in her hair, was loved by Poseidon

➕ 30B2

✉ 75km south of Kuşadası

☎ (0256) 813 1968

🕐 Daily 8:30–5:30

🍴 Two restaurants (£) opposite site entrance;

🚐 *Dolmuş*/minibus from Söke

♿ None

👆 Cheap

↔ Altınkum (➤ 64), Miletos (➤ 50), Priene (➤ 52)

❓ Tours from Kuşadası combine Miletos, Priene and Didyma

DİDİM (DIDYMA) ✪✪✪

This stupendous temple of Apollo, built to house an oracle, should not be missed. The Persians destroyed one temple here in the late 5th century BC, and the one that now looms dramatically by the side of the road was begun about 300 BC. A British archaeologist in the 19th century described the remains as 'piled up like shattered icebergs', but excellent restoration work has revealed the temple's mighty proportions and splendour. Be sure to walk to the back of the structure where one of the fallen columns has been preserved by archaeologists to show how it tumbled apart after falling. At the site entrance is an imposing head of Medusa, once part of a richly decorated frieze.

Steps lead up to the main platform and its twelve columns, and from here two tunnels lead down to the cellar. At the far side stood a small building where the cult statue resided. Here, next to the oracular spring, the prophetess delivered her utterances to the temple priests, who wrote them down and presented them to the client. Some fragments of the inscribed prophecies have been found but it is likely that most were destroyed by Christians who built a church inside the temple itself. The Romans built a stadium so close to the south that the bottom steps on this side of the temple were used as seats. Many names, carved on the seats to reserve places, can still be clearly made out. After visiting the temple, have a drink on the veranda of the Oracle pansiyon directly overlooking the west side of the site.

Fethiye

This walk starts at the tourist office (► 68) where a town map can be collected. After leaving the tourist office, turn right.

After 100m you will pass the town's Roman theatre on the right (► 68). At the roundabout just ahead, take the inland street, by following the black-on-yellow sign for the Altstadt.

You will soon pass a Turkish bath (► 115) and the Car Cemetery pub, opposite each other, while the Music Factory is a few doors down. At the end of the street have a look in the Ottoman Café (► 113).

Then turn left. Go down to the T-junction with the Atatürk statue and turn to the right, crossing to the other side of the street.

Just before the PTT (post office), a Lycian sarcophagus can be seen on the left (► 68).

Stay on the main road until a gleaming mosque is reached and at this junction turn right and walk up the cobbled street. At the T-junction, go left to follow the sign to the rock tombs, and cross to the other side. After a few hundred metres, turn right at another sign for the Lycian rock tombs, which come into view on the rock face ahead. Turn right at the top, and then left at the playground to walk up through houses to the site entrance for the tombs (► 25). To continue the walk, retrace your steps to the junction by the mosque and carry straight across and down Hastane Caddesi, towards the sea, and have lunch in the hotel.

Distance
5km

Time
2–3 hours

Start point
Tourist office
[map] 30C1

End point
Sesa Park Hotel
[map] 30C1

Lunch
Sesa Park Hotel
✉ Akdeniz Caddesi 17
☎ (0252) 614 4656

Cut into the rocky hillface overlooking Fethiye, some of the tombs can be reached on foot from the streets below

67

EUROMOS ❷❷

The only substantial remnant of the ancient city of Euromos is its temple of Zeus, but the setting among olive groves is so picturesque and the remains so evocative that it is well worth making the short detour if you are travelling between Milas and Kuşadası. Euromos was founded in the 6th century BC, and the temple owes its existence to the patronage of the Romans, probably the Emperor Hadrian (AD 117–38). The city itself was built half a kilometre to the northwest of the temple but there is little to see.

FETHİYE ❷❷

The modern town of Fethiye, occupying the site of ancient Telmessos, was completely rebuilt after a devastating earthquake in 1957, and the modern quayside and promenade stand on the rubble of the old city. There had been an earlier earthquake in 1857, so very little is left of ancient Telmessos. Nothing is known about its origins, but it became part of Lycia, fell to Alexander in due course and was later ruled by Rome. Apart from the Lycian rock tombs (➤ 25) and a recently excavated Roman theatre near the tourist office (both easily taken in on an early morning walk through town (➤ 67), the best reminder of ancient Telmessos is next to the post office in the centre of town. Here sits a large, double-fronted sarcophagus with an arched lid, carrying attractive reliefs of Lycian warriors. At the end of the 19th century it stood in the sea, but the falling of the sea level has returned it to dry ground.

Although Fethiye is clearly a resort town, it is quite different from Bodrum or Marmaris. Less sophisticated, it has managed to avoid intense commercialism, retaining a recognisably Turkish character.

Like Bodrum and Marmaris, however, it has a quayside that bustles with activity each morning as tourists take their seats for one of the popular boat excursions to nearby beaches and islands. It also has plenty of restaurants and hotels for visitors, lively bars, a Turkish bath (► 115), and lovely golden sandy beaches in the vicinity. Fethiye also makes a good base for visiting a number of major and minor ancient sites or for an excursion to the ghost town of Kayaköy (► 75).

There is a small **museum** in the centre of town with some interesting archaeological finds from Letoön and Patara. The main bus station is 2km to the east of the town, and a *dolmuş* station, in the centre of town behind the mosque, serves the local beaches. The bus company, 'Pamukkale', also has offices in the centre of town, so it is relatively straightforward to book long-distance bus journeys.

Ölüdeniz (► 21) is, justifiably, the most popular and famous of the local beaches but there are others near by at Calis and Hisarönü. There are twelve islands dotting Fethiye Bay, and boat trips visit some of these for swimming and exploring.

Left: the idyllic location adds charm to the Temple of Zeus at Euromas

Boat trips depart from Fethiye every morning

In the Know

If you only have a short time to visit western Turkey, or would like to get a real flavour of the region, here are some ideas:

10
Ways to Be a Local

Drink tea without milk throughout the day from tiny, tulip-shaped glasses.

Express a negative by slightly raising your head and eyes upwards and tutt-tutting.

Remove shoes before entering a mosque, and be modestly dressed. Women should cover their hair.

Relieve stress by using a set of worry beads.

Splash the proffered cologne around neck and face on long-distance buses.

Men should have a shave in a traditional hairdressing saloon.

Play backgammon on the street and be prepared for a return game.

Tolerate smoking, even in no-smoking areas. Turkey is a land of smokers.

Drink bottled mineral water rather than tap water, which tastes unpleasant.

Observe the Mediterranean custom of *piyasa vakti* ('plaza time') by dressing smartly, strolling through town and along the seafront in the evening, and indulging in aimless conversation.

10
Good Places to Have Lunch

Agora (£) Herakleia
☎ (0252) 543 5445
The smartest of the small number of restaurants in Herakleia, serving Turkish and some Western dishes in a pleasant outdoor setting under shade.

L'Angelo Italiano (£–££)
✉ Neyzen Tevfik Caddesi, Bodrum
☎ (0252) 614 63241
Situated inland at the marina side of town and consequently away from the crowds. Decent Italian dishes.

Efes Pub (£) ✉ SSK İşhani 07, Konak, İzmir
☎ (0232) 484 7036
🕐 8AM–midnight.
Conveniently close to the museums and bazaar, this licensed restaurant and bar. Good for lamb chops and steaks and a range of light salad-based meals.

İelgle (£) ✉ Güllübahçe
☎ (0256) 547 1009
The small waterfall alongside this restaurant adds to its charm. The menu offers fish dishes, kebabs, steak or meatballs. Ideal stopping point before or after a visit to ancient Priene.

Kalehan (£) ✉ Kalehan Hotel, Atatürk Caddesi 49, Selçuk ☎ (0232) 892 6154
The only restaurant in Selçuk with some character to its surroundings, plus the comfort of air-conditioning and good Turkish food. The à la carte menu changes daily, the four-course set meals are good value, and there is a wine list.

Körfez (£) ✉ Seafront, Çeşme ☎ (0232) 712 6718
This sea-facing restaurant has a large menu but it is the fish or fish-based dishes which are the most tempting. There is an impressive selection of *meze*, as well as the main fish dishes. There are also 'International cuisine selections' for those who prefer chicken curry or steak and chips.

Motel Koru (£) ✉ Pamukkale
☎ (0258) 272 2429
The restaurant in the Motel Koru overlooks the vast plains below the plateau of Pamukkale. The food is acceptable, but the big attraction is the view. There is a separate bar, just before the entrance to the restaurant.

Pergamum Pansiyon (£)
✉ Bankalar Caddesi 4, Bergama ☎ (0232) 633 2395

On the main street and less than 1km up from the tourist office on the same side of the street. Turkish meat and vegetable dishes waiting in steamtrays.

Rihtim (£) ✉ Çanakkale ☎ (0286) 217 1770

There are other restaurants alongside the Rihtim, but this is one of the longer-established places on the quayside street facing the Dardanelles, just to the left as you face main car ferry dock. The specialty is fish, served with salad and chips, but other dishes are on the menu.

Villa Pizza (£) ✉ Çarşi Caddesi Fethiye ☎ (0252) 614 6451

Choice of two dozen pizzas, half meat and half vegetarian. Around the corner from the Ottoman Café. For Turkish cuisine try to Meğri at No 13.

10
Top Activities

Boating: hire a boat, join a cruise or charter a boat with a crew.

Look under water: use a snorkel or dive – resorts have facilities for all levels of experience.

Swim: there is a huge choice of beaches (➤ 110).

Visit ancient sites: Ephesus and other popular sites have the most to see; less famous ones may have more atmosphere.

Visit a Greek island: for example Rhodes from Marmaris (➤ 82).

Walk: the best way to see the wildlife and landscape.

Shop: all day and half the night. Shops stay open late (➤ 104–9).

Watch the wildlife: loggerhead turtles on beaches, storks on buildings, lizards and tortoises at ancient sites, wild flowers everywhere.

Enjoy the nightlife: summer is a non-stop party at the big resorts.

Watch the arcane art of camel wrestling: usually between late October and March, especially popular in the Selçuk area.

10
Best Buys

• Carpets are sold everywhere
• Ceramic plates, bowls, jugs and pots come in vivid blues and greens with abstract designs
• A brass tea tray, complete with tiny tea glasses
• Designer-label clothes
• Food: pine-scented honey, bags of pine nuts, gift-wrapped pastries and Turkish delight
• Leather jackets, coats, shoes, bags and belts
• Meerschaum is a soft white magnesium silicate

Relieve stress with a set of worry beads

from western Anatolia, carved by craftsmen into pipes and figurines
• Onyx is best purchased from a workshop where you see the quartz being cut and shaped. Inexpensive, but very heavy
• Ottoman-style memento, such as a water pipe, copperware or jewellery
• *Raki*: a bottle or two

Boat trips in a gulet are available from most coastal resorts

GÖKOVA KÖRFEZI (GULF OF GÖKOVA)

🕇 30B2

✉ Between Bodrum and
Marmaris

🚢 Boats and yachts from
Bodrum and Marmaris

🎫 Moderate to expensive,
depending on the length
of cruise

↔ Bodrum (➤ 58–62),
Marmaris (➤ 80–1)

Bodrum is the most popular departure point for a
'turquoise cruise' or 'blue voyage' along the beautiful,
56km-long stretch of coast of the Gulf of Gökova. *Gülets*,
the traditional broad-beamed vessels of the area, can be
chartered with a crew, and watersports equipment is
usually included. Destinations include Yedi Adalar, a quiet
bay on the southeast corner of the gulf and Sideyri Adası
(Cedar Island, ➤ 85), with the beach that Anthony is
supposed to have created for Cleopatra.

GÜMBET ✪

🕇 30B2

✉ 2km west of Bodrum

🍴 Plenty of tourist
restaurants (£–££)

🚌 *Dolmuş*/minibus from
Bodrum

↔ Bodrum (➤ 58–62),
Gümüşlük (➤ 73),
Turgutreis (➤ 89)

This beach, the closest one to Bodrum, has become a self-
contained resort, and is very popular with young people,
(the British especially), on a two-week package holiday.
There are hotels, pubs, discos and restaurants in
abundance; the 600m long beach is not superb but even
so you cannot be sure of finding a space in high summer.
The best thing about Gümbet is the range of water-based
sports and activities available on the beach.

GÜMÜŞLÜK   ○○

A photogenic fishing village, half an hour's drive from Bodrum, Gümüşlük has mercifully escaped the worst excesses of tourism. The village is on the site of ancient Myndos and this has resulted in restrictions being imposed on new buildings. The fish restaurants (➤ 98) along the waterfront are not cheap but they make a delightful stop for lunch or a sunset dinner. The 1km-long beach is a mixture of sand and gravel, and swimming in the sea at the south end brings you very close to some Myndos ruins.

➕ 30B2
✉ 15km west of Bodrum
🍴 Fish restaurants (££–£££)
🚌 Dolmuş/minibus from Bodrum
↔ Bodrum (➤ 58–62), Turgutreis (➤ 89), Yalıkavak (➤ 90), Gümbet (➤ 72), Ortakent (➤ 84)

HISARÖNÜ AND OVACIK   ○

Hisarönü and Ovacık are close to the coast though not actually on it, and are busily developing as accommodation centres for the Fethiye region. Hisarönü, the larger and more popular of the two resorts, is very much a tourist satellite settlement for Ölüdeniz, just 4km away down the hillside. Fish and chip shops testify to Hisarönü's popularity with the British; for a quieter destination nearby Calis (➤ 64) would be preferable. New bars and restaurants are opening in both Hisarönü and Ovacık, with a better choice of fare than the eating places on the beaches.

➕ 30C1
✉ 10km south of Fethiye
🍴 Bars and restaurants (£–££)
🚌 Dolmuş/minibus from Fethiye
↔ Kayaköy (➤ 75) Ölüdeniz (➤ 21), Calis (➤ 64), Lycian Rock Tombs (➤ 25), Xanthos (➤ 26), Letoön (➤ 77), Pınara (➤ 85), Tlos (➤ 88)

IASOS   ○

Populated from around 2000 BC, ancient Iasos prospered under the Romans, and in Byzantine times the Knights of St John built a castle here. The last vestiges of the town lie by the side of the village of Kıyıkışlacık, whose name translates as 'the little barracks on the coast'. Most of what can still be seen belongs to the 2nd century AD, including the remains of a Roman mausoleum and a bouleuterion (meeting hall), but it takes a leap of the imagination to picture them in their complete state. The Byzantine castle is the most impressive sight and gives fine views. A small museum stands over the mausoleum, and its fragmented exhibits found on the site are poignant reminders of the almost-vanished town.

➕ 30B2
✉ Kıyıkışlacık, 8km north west of Milas, 4km southeast of Euromos
🕐 Open 24 hours
🍴 Fish restaurants (£) in Kıyıkışlacık
🚌 Dolmuş/minibus from Milas or boat from Güllük
💷 Cheap
↔ Milas (➤ 83), Euromos (➤ 68)

Left: Diners can get their feet wet at the fish restaurants in Gümüşlük

➕ 30B2
✉ 8km south of Marmaris
🍴 Tourist restaurants (£–££)
are easy to find
🚌 *Dolmuş*/minibus, or ferry
dolmuş, from Marmaris
↔ Marmaris (➤ 80–1),
Turunç (➤ 89), Bozburun
(➤ 64), Datça (➤ 65),
Ródos (Rhodes, ➤ 82)

*İçmeler is a quieter
place than its near
neighbour Marmaris*

İÇMELER ✪

The gap between Marmaris and the resort of İçmeler
is getting smaller all the time, but there is still a qualitative
difference between the two towns. İçmeler has a
more sedate character: the discos tend to close earlier,
there is little in the way of budget accommodation, and
the typical summer visitor – probably British or German – is
more likely to be middle-aged. An 8km beach links
the two resorts. Despite it being municipal property
and open to all, most of the hotels backing onto the beach
try to claim a patch by filling it with their deckchairs. You
can make the half-hour journey by *dolmuş* ferry, the last
stop from Marmaris being at the back of the Munumar
Vista hotel (➤ 103).

KALKAN ✪✪

Coming from Fethiye, the road suddenly arrives at the top of a cliff and looks down to a little town hugging the cliffside in the curve of a bay. A well-kept secret amongst seasoned budget travellers until tourism made its impact in the early 1980s, Kalkan is still a pleasant, and more sophisticated, alternative to Fethiye as a base for exploring this corner of the coast. The town's picturesque houses seem precariously attached to the hillside and there are steep cobbled streets, a pebble-beached cove, a good range of accommodation and decent restaurants as well.

🔲 30C1
✉ 80km east of Fethiye
🍴 Restaurants (£–££)
🚌 Dolmuş/minibus from Fethiye and Kas
♿ None: steep streets are unavoidable
↔ Xanthos (➤ 26), Letoön (➤ 77), Pınara (➤ 85), Tlos (➤ 88)

KAUNOS ✪

Ancient Kaunos was founded in the 9th century BC, and its ruins make an worthwhile excursion by boat from nearby Dalyan. Originally a Carian city, Kaunos came under the cultural influence of neighbouring Lycia, and this is apparent in its decorated rock tombs, which resemble the Lycian tombs at Fethiye (➤ 25). Archaeological work is still going on at Kaunos; the ruins include well-preserved sections of wall from the 4th century BC, and a theatre which was built some two hundred years later. In ancient

🔲 30C2
✉ Dalyan (➤ 65)
🕤 8:30–5:30
🚌 Dolmuş/minibus from Marmaris, Muğla and Fethiye
💷 Cheap
↔ Dalyan (➤ 65), Köyceğiz (➤ 76)
❓ Day tours from Dalyan

times the Mediterranean came right up to the acropolis but the marshland that now attracts mosquitoes (bring repellent) must have been in evidence in the past: Herodotus noted that the inhabitants were reputed to have yellowish skin, probably caused by malaria.

The rock tombs of Kaunos are best seen on one of the regular boat trips

KAYAKÖY ✪✪

This town of some 2,000 homes, once called Levissi, lost its Greek Orthodox inhabitants in 1923 in the exchange of populations that followed the War of Independence (➤ 11). An attempt to turn the place into a holiday village has been successfully squashed and it remains uninhabited, a place in which to wander and ponder the human cost of politics.

🔲 30C1
✉ 7km south of Fethiye
🍴 Restaurants and cafés (£)
🚌 Dolmuş/minibus from Fethiye
↔ Fethiye (➤ 68–9), Ölüdeniz (➤ 21), Calis (➤ 64), Hisarönü (➤ 73)

KNİDOS ✪

📌 30B2
✉ 35km west of Datça
🕐 8–7
🍴 Fish restaurants (£–££) near dock
🚌 Boat from Datça
♿ None
💷 Cheap
🔄 Datça (► 65)

Below: *ruined Knidos has a dramatic location*

The location is an appealing one – the exposed tip of the spiny Marmaris peninsula – and the ancient city of Cnidus was built here to benefit the Mediterranean sea trade. The settlement grew rich and famous, and at one time its proudest boast was a statue of Aphrodite, carved by Praxiteles, the Michelangelo of his time. The statue has disappeared but there are various remnants of the old city, spread over a wide area: the most substantial are the Hellenistic theatre and the Byzantine basilicas, and you can also see the remains of a lighthouse and necropolis. The view is spellbinding, with a number of the Greek islands, Ródos (Rhodes), Cos, Yiali, Nisiros and Khalki all visible from the ruins. A rough road leads to Knidos (► 63), but it is much more pleasant to take a boat from Datça. Day-long boat trips include stops for lunch and a swim.

Did you know ?

The statue of Aphrodite that once adorned Knidos was a major tourist attraction in its time. It was considered to be one of the world's finest works of art and may have been the first free-standing sculpture of a female nude in Greece. It is thought to have been destroyed by Christians in the Byzantine era; copies survive in European cities and New York.

KÖYCEĞİZ ✪

📌 30C2
✉ 50km east of the Muğla–Marmaris road
🍴 Restaurants (£–££)
🚌 *Dolmuş*/minibus from Marmaris and Muğla
ℹ Main square ☎ (0252) 262 4703 🕐 Mon–Fri 8:30–12:30
🔄 Dalyan (► 65) Kaunos (► 75)

A peaceful inland town on Lake Köyceğiz, without the intense commercialism of coastal resorts, Köyceğiz has a modest appeal that pleases many visitors. The lake is the centre of attraction and there are regular boat excursions to the opposite shore, where visitors can bathe in the life-enhancing mud of the Sultaniye Kaplıcaları. These thermal baths, rich in calcium, potassium and sulphur, attract far fewer visitors than those at Ilıca and also benefit from a more interesting setting. Boats also go down the lake to Daylan and Kaunos: ask at the tourist office in the main square for details.

LABRANDA ⚫⚫

The sanctuary of Zeus at Labranda is not easy to reach, even with your own car, but the effort is richly rewarded. A few miles outside Milas, on the main road heading north to Selçuk, the turn-off is signposted on the right. The site is 14km further on, and the paved road ends after 6km at the village of Karigeak. It is not advisable to try the drive in winter unless it is very dry. A Swedish group of archaeologists has done some work here at Labranda, and the main ruins are clearly marked. The most interesting are the two structures where devotees held their sacrificial banquets, and an impressive 4th-century BC tomb. The isolated setting and the sweeping views afforded by the steep location of these little-visited ruins make this one of the more evocative ancient sites of the Turkish Aegean.

🟦 30B2
✉️ 17km north of Milas
🕐 8–8
🚌 Car or taxi from Milas
♿ None
💲 Cheap
🔁 Euromos (► 68), Iasos (► 73), Milas (► 83)

LETOÖN ⭐

Letoön, the Lycian centre for the worship of Leto, was an important sanctuary in ancient times. First excavated in 1962, the remains of three 3rd-century BC temples, dedicated to Leto, Artemis and Apollo, bear testimony to its significance. Leto was a nymph who was loved by Zeus, and was jealously hounded by his wife Hera as a consequence. Wolves guided the preganant Leto to the River Xanthos, where she bathed and renamed the place Lycia (from the Greek for wolf, *lykos*) before giving birth to Artemis and Apollo. Alexander the Great came here and received encouragement for his imminent battle against the Persians. There is also a well-preserved Hellenistic theatre and an inscription found here was very important in the eventual deciphering of the Lycian language.

🟦 30C1
✉️ Kumluova, 6km southwest of Xanthos
🕐 8:30–5
🚌 *Dolmuş*/minibus frôm Fethiye to Kumluova
♿ None
💲 Cheap
🔁 Xanthos (► 26, 90), Kalkan (► 75), Pinara (► 85), Tlos (► 88)

Letoön was the most important religious centre in ancient Lycia

Marmaris to Pamukkale

Leave Marmaris, following the signs for Muğla.

About 12km after passing the right turn for Fethiye, the road climbs through a mountain pass to reach Muğla, and there are splendid views of the Gulf of Gökova.

As you approach the ring road at Muğla, follow the signs to Denizli.

The road (330) to Denizli is over 100km along a scenic route which is very much off the beaten tourist track. The changing colours of the landscape as the road weaves its way towards the village of Kale are enchanting.

Distance
150km (excluding Aphrodisias)

Time
4–5 hours

Start Point
Marmaris
✚ 30B2

End Point
Pamukkale
✚ 30C3

Lunch
Motel Koru (➤ 70)

The road heads on to Tavas. Turn left if you want to make a diversion (60km return) to Aphrodisias (➤ 34). Follow the Afyon/Ankara road out of Denizli and after about 8km take the left turn, signposted for Pamukkale.

Very soon after this turning, just before the village of Korucuk, there is a left turning signposted for Laodiceia (➤ 49). Save this visit for later and press on for Pamukkale (➤ 22–3). This is the best place for lunch, after which you can explore Hierapolis (➤ 20).

In the evening, if time allows, it does not take long to drive down to Laodiceia. If you turn left onto the main road in the direction of Ankara, it is less than 2km to a crumbling old caravanserai on the left side of the road as you reach the bottom of a hill.

Left: *social life on the beach and, above, time yourself at a classical site*

7

Mooring space is at a premium in Marmaris harbour

MARMARİS ✪✪

Set by the side of an 8km-long bay and framed by pine forests and oleander shrubs, Marmaris looks out to sea where the Aegean and the Mediterranean meet. The town's name is said to come from a remark by Süleyman the Magnificent in 1522 – *mimari* translates as 'hang the architect'. He was unimpressed by the fortress he was using for an attack on the Knights of St John at Rhodes. In 1798, the British Admiral Nelson used the 3km-wide bay to prepare his fleet for an attack on the French at Abukir.

Along with Kuşadası and Bodrum, this is one of the big three coastal resorts on the Turkish Aegean, and manages to satisfy most modern visitors. There is a strong contingent of young people who are here to party, and as in Kuşadası, one of the roads has become known as Bar Street. Families come here on package holidays, which often include free accommodation for children, and many of the hotels have a children's pool and play area. Marmaris also has a very large and modern marina with a highly affluent clientele, hence the expensive restaurants around town. Other visitors find that neighbouring İçmeler, now virtually a suburb, is ideal as a quieter accommodation base, while still being handy for shopping in Marmaris and sightseeing in the area.

Choose a carpet carefully and take the sales talk with a pinch of salt

The town may lack Bodrum's air of sophistication, but a stroll along the promenade at dusk does have its charms. Islands and coves can be made out in the bay, scores of brightly painted boats nod at their moorings, and chains of twinkling lights enhance the scene. Restaurants, bars and cafés line the pedestrianised road and tempt you to take a seat under the palm trees.

The statue of Atatürk near the waterfront is the hub of the town centre. The statue divides the two main streets that face the harbour, Atatürk Caddesi to the west and Kordon Caddesi to the east. The main inland road that comes down to meet the statue is Ulusal Egemenlik Bulvarı. Most places of interest to the visitor are to the east of the statue, and Kordon Caddesi leads to the tourist office, banks, post office and shops.

There is a small, uninspiring **museum** behind the tourist office, but most visitors prefer to check out the shops or organise day trips to the nearby islands of Rhodes, Kaunos or Knidos and numerous other destinations, by sea or land.

🔲 30B2
✉ 170km west of Fethiye, 165km east of Bodrum
🍴 Restaurants (£–£££)
🚌 Buses from Bodrum, Fethiye, İzmir, Pamukkale
ℹ️ Iskele Meydanı
   ☎ (0252) 412 1035
   🕐 Summer, 8–7:30; winter Mon–Fri 8–12, 1–5
↔ İçmeler (➤ 74), Turunç (➤ 89), Bozburun (➤ 64), Datça (➤ 65), Rhodes (➤ 82)

Museum

🕐 8–12, 1–5
💷 Cheap

Distinctive blue and white beehives produce some of Turkey's best honey

Did you know ?

The lines of blue and white beehives in the Marmaris area (➤ 63), usually lying flat on the ground, produce some of the best honey in the whole of Turkey. Be sure to sample the dark-coloured çam balı variety, distinguished by its pine scent that derives from the forests where the hives are placed.

Ródos (Rhodes)

Distance
Approx 80km return trip

Time
Crossing takes 45 minutes.
Allow all day to explore town

Start/end point
Marmaris Harbour
✚ 30B2

Lunch
Plenty of choice (£–££)

ℹ️ City of Rhodes Tourist
Office ☎ (0241) 35945
🕐 Daily 8:30AM–9PM

❓ With a day return ticket
there are no taxes to pay
and you don't need a visa.
Take your passport,
though, and don't forget
to check the times of the
last trip back.

Take the hydrofoil from Marmaris harbour. You can buy tickets in advance from one of the travel agencies on Kordon Caddesi.

The 45-minute journey will take you to the Mandraki harbour in the more modern part of Rhodes Town, the capital of this popular Greek island. The Colossus of Rhodes, one of the Seven Wonders of the Ancient World, is believed to have stood over the entrance to this harbour.

After disembarking make your way to the tourist office in the Plateía Riminí, just north of the medieval town.

From here you can explore the old town, mainly a product of occupation by the Knights Hospitallers of St John. They occupied the island from 1306 (after losing control of Jerusalem) to 1522, when they capitulated to Süleyman the Magnificent's Turkish army after a seige lasting for 177 days. As well touring the medieval walls, the Palace of the Grand Masters and the Byzantine and Archaeological Museums are well worth a visit. There are plenty of fascinating mosques, old streets and scores of shopping opportunities to keep you occupied all day.

When you have had enough of the bustle, return to the harbour for the hydrofoil back to Marmaris.

There are many quiet alleys in the medieval quarter of Rhodes Town

MİLAS ✪

This agricultural town was the site of ancient Mylasa and capital of the Carian kingdom. It's worth following the main street, Kadıağa Caddesi, which becomes Gümüşkesen Caddesi, to reach the large Roman tomb known as the Gümüşkesen about 1km west of the town centre. It may be a copy on a smaller scale of the Mausoleum of Halicarnassus (Bodrum, ► 61). Retrace your route to the very beginning of Kadıağa Caddesi, at the east side of town near the canal, where there is a very attractive 14th-century mosque, the Ulu Cami. Follow the road going north from here for about 250m, and the Baltalı Kapı will come into view. Known as the Gate with an Axe, this well-preserved Roman gate has a double-headed axe carved into a stone on the north side.

🚩 30B2
✉ 45km northeast of Bodrum
🍴 Restaurants (£)
🚌 Buses from Marmaris and Kuşadası
↔ Euromos (► 68), Iasos (► 73), Labranda (► 77)

MUĞLA ✪

Start by calling at the tourist office and collecting a town map; this is a town to walk around at a leisurely pace, taking in the general air of prosperity. The most interesting area to explore is the old Ottoman quarter, with its winding streets of picturesque buildings. From the tourist office by the Atatürk statue on the central roundabout, head north up Kurşunlu Caddesi and take a look in at Yağcıar Hanı, a modern shopping centre in a converted caravanserai. The street continues north up to the town's bazaar, also worth visiting, and higher up on the hillside are many photogenic houses. These are well-preserved examples of domestic Ottoman architecture.

🚩 30C2
✉ 73km north of Marmaris
🍴 Restaurants (£) in the centre of town
🚌 Dolmuş/minibus to Bodrum, Denizli, İzmir, Marmaris
ℹ Central roundabout with Atatürk statue
☎ (0252) 214 3127
🕐 Summer Mon–Fri 8–7; winter Mon–Fri 8–12, 1–5

ÖLÜDENIZ (► 21, TOP TEN)

One of the many attractive examples of Ottoman architecture in Muğla

ÖREN ✪

☩ 30B2
✉ 55km south of Milas
🍽 Restaurants (£) near beach
🚌 Occasional *dolmuş*/minibus from Milas

Byzantine Fortress
🕐 8AM–dusk
💰 Cheap

It is easy to miss Ören: after leaving Milas and travelling south for 3km, look for the main junction where the road goes right for Bodrum. Turn left instead for Muğla; the turn for Ören is very soon after on the right. Ören is a pleasant coastal village, used more by Turkish families than foreign holidaymakers, with an attractive 1km-long pebbly beach, and the scant remains of the ancient city of Ceramus. Public transport is infrequent, and it is best to drive yourself. The **Byzantine fortress** here is a good place for a picnic.

ORTAKENT ✪

☩ 30B2
✉ 10km west of Bodrum
🍽 Restaurants (£–££)
🚌 *Dolmuş*/minibus to Bodrum
↔ Bodrum (➤ 58–62), Gümüşlük (➤ 73), Turgutreis (➤ 89)

One of the better beaches on the Bodrum peninsula, Ortakent's sand stretches for 2km. The road is closed to traffic, so it is a safe place for children. There is nothing to see or do here but enjoy the sun, sand and sea. Various watersports are available, but the windsurfing is as exciting as it gets here. Ortakent has become popular on a small scale with British package groups.

PATARA ✪✪

☩ 30C1
✉ 7km south of Xanthos
🕐 Summer 7:30–7; winter 8:30–5 (ancient site)
🍽 Restaurants (£) on beach
🚌 *Dolmuş*/minibus to Fethiye and Kalkan
♿ None (ancient site)
💰 Cheap (ancient site)
↔ Xanthos (➤ 26 and 90), Letoön (➤ 77)

A very wide 8km-long, sandy beach is the great attraction of Patara. Its gleaming white expanse is also a conservation area for birds and turtles, so the beach closes at dusk. Be cautious when swimming: there are some strong currents. The ruins of ancient Patara, an important supply base for the Romans, are 1km away. It was a port, but sand has engulfed the harbour and buildings. The highlight is undoubtedly the sand-filled theatre.

Patara has one of the best beaches in Turkey

PINARA ⭐

This is not an easy to place to reach, even with your own transport, but the journey is attractive, and lets you indulge in the illusion that you have just discovered ancient Pınara yourself. Very little is known about the place, except that it was an important Lycian city that minted its own coins. The most compelling spectacle is the openings cut into in the huge mass of rock that towers over the site. They are thought to be tombs, but access is impossible to all but dedicated rockclimbers and should not be attempted.There are other tombs at ground level and the most interesting of these, known as the Royal Tomb, displays fine reliefs showing people and walled settlements. Of the other ruins, the theatre is the best preserved. Bus travellers have to walk the last 5km from the Pınara turning.

SIDEYRI ADASI (CEDAR ISLAND) ⭐

Legend has it that Mark Anthony transported all the fine sand on the beach from northern Africa, as a personal gift to the Egyptian queen: hence the name Cleopatra's beach. The beach is the main attraction for the many people who visit on day excursions from Marmaris and Bodrum. Tours from Marmaris include road transport to the boat at Çamli İskelesi. The island's name comes from the ancient city of Cedrae. It was sacked by the Spartans during the 5th-century BC Peloponnesian War, and retained its Greek culture until Arab invasions in the 7th century AD.

➕ 30C1
✉ 46km south-east of Fethiye
🕐 Open 24 hours
🍴 Snacks (£) 2km
🚌 *Dolmuş*/minibus from Fethiye to Pınara turning
♿ None
💵 Cheap
↔ Tlos (➤ 88), Sidyma (➤ 88), Xanthos (➤ 16, 90)

Above: *a distinctive 'gothic' sarcophagus at ancient Pınara*

➕ 30B2
✉ Gulf of Gökova
🚌 Boats from Taşbükü and Çamli İskelesi
↔ Gulf of Gökova (➤ 72)
❓ Tours from Marmaris include road transport to Çamli İskelesi

Food & Drink

Turkish cuisine has been open to various influences, a legacy of the far-reaching Ottoman Empire, but the underlying character-istic is a determination to conserve the natural tastes of fresh

ingredients. The country imports very little food: meat, fruit and vegetables, honey and jam are all produced in Turkey.

Above: *water-melons are abundant in Turkey*

Right: *a visit to a restaurant serving regional cuisine will surprise and delight*

Bread with Everything
White bread is ubiquitous – it is served with breakfast, lunch and dinner. When fresh it is soft and palatable but it soon becomes stale. Brown bread is difficult to find in the coastal resorts, but it exists and is worth seeking out in bakeries.

Meals of the Day

Breakfast in Turkey usually consists of bread, honey, sheep's cheese and olives, served with tea. Depending on the class of hotel, the more substantial English or American breakfast may receive token acknowledgment in the form of cereals, cooked eggs and ham. Lunch is also a relatively light affair, evening dinner being the main meal of the day. The traditional starters take the form of delicious hot and cold *meze* – small dishes using a variety of ingredients, for example puréed aubergines (*patlıcan salatası*), stuffed vine leaves (*zeytinagli yaprak dolması*), and finely rolled cheese pastries (*sigara böreği*). Main dishes are usually based around lamb or beef, although boiled chicken (*tavuk*) and roast chicken (*pilav*) are also popular. Restaurants usually have fresh fish on the menus such as turbot, bream, bass, mussels and crab. Sweet desserts are highly appreciated in Turkey, and can be glorious: baklava (puff pastry with syrup, and filled with nuts), custard-based desserts and rice puddings are all favourites.

Above: sweet, sticky desserts are very popular

Restaurants

There are two main types of restaurants: the plain *lokanta* and the more formal *restoran*. The *lokanta* keeps its warm, previously cooked, dishes on display in steam trays. The fare is simple but filling, usually consisting of stews, stuffed peppers, beans and rice. A *restoran* should offer a range of courses (*meze*, soup, meat dishes and desserts) and, unlike the average *lokanta*, will also serve beer and wine. There are also specialist restaurants, the names of which will indicate their specialty. The *pide salonu*, or *pideci*, offers pitta bread with various fillings, the *köftesi* serves meatballs, and the *kebapçı* concentrates on roast meat.

Something to Drink?

Tea (*çay*) is drunk throughout the day, served in tiny, gold-rimmed glasses and without milk. Apple tea (*elma çay*) is a particular favourite with the proprietors of carpet shops who wish to make potential customers feel welcome. Turkish coffee is not as common as one might expect. Turkish people drink it, in various degrees of sweetness (*sade* is without sugar, *az* and *orta* are medium, while *çok* is saturated in sugar). The national alcoholic drink is *raki* (➤ 98), but Turkish wine is widely available in shops and licensed restaurants. The less expensive brands will not suit everyone's palate. Locally brewed beer (*bira*) is readily available, and the Efes brand is deservedly popular with both locals and visitors. Domestically produced gin (*cin*), vodka (*vokta*) and cognac (*kanyak*) are less expensive than imported products but, other than in cocktails, the difference in taste is significant.

Turkish tea is difficult to avoid

Above: *the ruins at Tlos reflect an unusually mixed heritage*

SIDYMA ✪

This is the least visited of the Lycian sites because there is no public transport. What can be seen mostly dates back to Roman times, although there are some Lycian rock-cut tombs, a pillar tomb that has lost its grave-chamber from the top and an interesting row of sarcophagi. The site is always open.

TLOS ✪✪

Ancient Tlos was one of the more important Lycian cities, and in the 19th century it became a winter headquarters for a pirate called Kanli Ali Ağa. The ruins reflect this mixed parentage. The empty remains of the pirate's fortress tower over the site from the top of the acropolis, and the Lycian remains include rock-cut tombs. If the attendant is around, ask for help in locating the best preserved one, which has an Ionic temple façade and a relief of Bellerophon riding the winged horse Pegasus. The theatre is also in good condition; the baths are the most interesting of the other scattered remains.

TURGUTREİS ✪

Turgutreis is totally dedicated to tourism, and package holiday hotels abound. There are well over a hundred restaurants, and a sufficient number of bars and nightclubs to keep visitors amused for a week or longer. The parasol-peppered beach has coarse sand and, because the sea remains shallow for quite some way out, is suitable for young children.

🞢 30B2
✉ 20km west of Bodrum
🍴 Restaurants (£–££)
🚌 *Dolmuş*/minibus from Bodrum
🔁 Bodrum (➤ 58–62), Gümüşlük (➤ 73), Yalıkavak (➤ 90), Gümbet (➤ 72)

TURUNÇ ✪

Turunç used to be a place to escape from the crowds of Marmaris. Tourist brochures still portray the modern resort as a relaxing hideaway, but this is stretching the truth a little. The 500m beach of coarse sand, with a splendid backdrop of cliffs and pine trees, is the focus of daily activity. It is safe for swimming and you can hire watersports equipment. Water taxis are always bobbing next to the jetties, waiting to take people to coves along the coast.

🞢 30B2
✉ 10km south of Marmaris
🍴 Restaurants (£–££)
🚌 *Dolmuş*/minibus fromr water *dolmuş* to Marmaris
🔁 İçmeler (➤ 74), Bozburun (➤ 64), Datça (➤ 65), Marmaris (➤ 80–1) Rhodes (➤ 82)

> ### *Did you know ?*
>
> *Some of the most enjoyable specialist guides to the ancient sites of western Turkey are* Turkey Beyond the Meander, Lycian Turkey *and* Aegean Turkey, *written by George E Bean in the 1960s.*

Turunç is easily reached from Marmaris by minibus or water dolmuş

XANTHOS

From the modern village of Kınık, on the main Fethiye-Kalkan road, it is a five-minute walk to the ancient Lycian capital of Xanthos (➤ 26). The acropolis overlooks the Eşen Çayi river, and it is easy to imagine the Lycians looking down on the plain in the 6th century BC as a Persian army advanced on their citadel. Rather than surrender, they set fire to their city, and those who did not die fighting perished in the flames. The ruins of the new city that arose in the 5th century BC are now the major attraction. In 42 BC the Roman general Brutus attacked the city only to be confronted by another act of mass suicide as the Lycians realized that defeat was imminent. Under Roman rule the city thrived again, and in Byzantine times it was a centre of Christianity. A path near the toilets leads to the remains of a Byzantine church, a pleasant lunch spot.

YALIKAVAK ✪

*Looking out to sea from
Yalıkavak's old windmill*

Tucked away on the northern shore, this is one of the less-developed of the many resorts on the Bodrum peninsula. The small town is pretty in a manicured kind of way, with a restored 300-year-old windmill in the middle of a pedestrianised area of cobbled streets. There are far better beaches on the peninsula than Yalıkavak's pebbly one, and this helps to keep the crowds away (choose a hotel with a pool if you are staying here). Yalıkavak is ideal for people who want the facilities of bigger resorts, but not the non-stop nightlife.

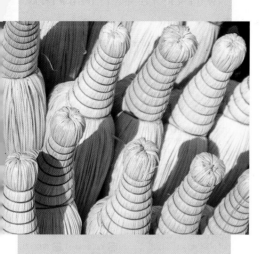

Where To...

Above: *brooms for sale in İzmir's bazaar*
Right: *belly dancing, like this show in Çeşme, is featured in many coastal resorts*

91

Northern Aegean

Prices

Approximate prices for a three-course meal for one person are shown by a £ symbol:

£ = budget, under 2 million lire
££ = moderate, 2–4 million lire
£££ = expensive, over 4 million lire

Ayvalık

Öz Canlibalik (££–£££)

There are a number of quality fish restaurants in Ayvalık and this is one of the best. It is close to the seafront and will have whatever local fish have been recently brought in. Ask about the availability of *kidonia* and *ayvada*, two types of mussel which do not often appear on the menus of restaurants in the eastern Mediterranean. The *meze* here are also recommended.

✉ Gazinolar Caddesi
🕓 Lunch and dinner
🚌 *Dolmuş*/minibus from Çanakkale, Assos, Bergama, İzmir

Bergama

Sağlam (£–££)

On the main street in the centre of town, not far from the tourist office. At lunch time there are the standard hot dishes waiting in steamtrays, but it is also worth asking about the regional dishes from Urfa. There is a small courtyard at the back for alfresco dining, and rooms upstairs.

✉ Cumhuriyet Meydanı 29
☎ (0232) 632 8897 🕓 8–8

Çanakkale

Aussie & Kiwi (£)

The name, the free 'Milo' with meals and the Vegemite draw in Australians and New Zealanders, but anyone seeking dishes such as apple crumble or a hearty breakfast will warm to this place. Fish is the best bet for a main meal. Check out the restaurant's book for comments by customers on the food, Turkey and life in general. Lies at the military museum end of town.

✉ Yali Caddesi 32 ☎ (0286) 212 1722 🕓 8AM–2PM

Karakas (£–££)

A large menu of fish and meat dishes in a pleasant and clean restaurant which is patronised by locals as well as visitors. Licensed.

✉ Yali Caddesi ☎ (0286) 217 6140 🕓 8:30AM–11PM

Trakya (£)

This restaurant has two outlets, one on each side of a square facing the main docking area where ferries cross the Dardanelles. These are *lokanta* restaurants (► 87) and ordering is simply a matter of pointing at whatever takes your fancy on the steamtrays. Delicious food, served with mountains of bread, and inexpensive.

✉ Demircioğlu Caddesi
☎ (0286) 217 7257
🕓 8AM–9PM

Çeşme

Chefs Palace (££)

Brightly lit at night, the restaurant is easy to find in the middle of town near the sea. The speciality is Mediterranean cuisine but there are also Turkish dishes and a selection of vegetarian choices.

✉ Sakarya Mh. Memis Sk. 10
☎ (0232) 7128150 🕓 8:30AM–10:30PM

Dost Pide & Pizza (£–££)

A bright and cheerful tourist restaurant in Ilica, 4km west of Çeşme, with tables filling the pavement. As well as the pizzas, there is also a variety of meat dishes on the menu.

✉ **İifne Caddesi, Ilica**

☎ **(0232) 723 2059**

🕐 **8AM–late** 🚌 *Dolmuş* to Çeşme

Sahíl (£–££)

This is a typical Çeşme restaurant facing the sea, with indoor and outdoor tables, and a menu that has both Turkish and European dishes including kebabs and pizza. The Sahíl was established in 1954, and is one of the oldest restaurants catering for visitors.

✉ **Cumhuriyet Meydanı 13**

☎ **(0232) 712 8294**

🕐 **8AM–11PM**

İzmir

Café Cine (£)

A modernist-style café, with green tables and the menu written on a blackboard. Standard dishes include spaghetti bolognese and macaroni with cheese sauce. Easy to find because the street is just behind the Hilton Hotel, and a cinema is next door.

✉ **1379 Sokak 57/B** ☎ **(0232) 446 0637** 🕐 **9AM–9:30PM**

🚌 **62, 68, 77**

Chinese Restaurant (££)

Situated down a street behind the Hilton hotel, this licensed restaurant has a long menu of beef, chicken, duck, seafood, rice and noodle dishes. The cook's specials include a hot cabbage salad, lamb with green onion, fried chicken with orange sauce and steamed dumpling. Take-away service available.

✉ **1379 Sokak** ☎ **(0232) 483 0079** 🕐 **Lunch and dinner**

🚌 **62, 68, 77**

Collanade (£££)

Excellent Mediterranean cuisine in the comfort of the Hilton hotel, with evening buffets and à la carte lunches. Theme nights – Chinese, Turkish and others – sometimes dictate the nature of the food so it is advisable to check what's on.

✉ **Hilton Hotel, Gazi Paça Pasa Bulvarı** ☎ **(0232) 441 6060** 🚌 **12–11PM** 🚌 **61–63, 116, 110, 112, 150**

Deniz (££–£££)

The Deniz specialises in fish dishes, and is regarded as the best fish restaurant in town. You may need to make a reservation to secure one of the outdoor tables. Popular with business people during the week, less formal at weekends.

✉ **Atatürk Caddesi 188-B**

☎ **(0232) 422 0601** 🕐 **Lunch and dinner**

Fast Fish (£)

A modern fast food-style place with food served in plastic boxes. No meat dishes but a variety of fish fillet burgers, kalamari, fish balls, seafood soup and seafood salads. Cheap and suitable for a quick lunch.

✉ **1379 Sokak** ☎ **(0232) 445 3795/2059** 🕐 **9AM–9:30PM**

🚌 **62, 68, 77**

Seçkin (£)

In the centre of town, with a good choice of Turkish pizzas, grills and pastries, and an upstairs area with half a dozen computers and access to e-mail and the Internet, paid for by the half-hour.

✉ **M Kemalettin Caddesi 16/A, Konak** ☎ **(0232) 489 2404**

🕐 **8AM–late** 🚌 **several**

Turkish (Vegetarian) Delight

At the Buğay restaurant in Bodrum try a light lunch of salad with excellent brown breads, based on Turkish village recipes, or the breakfast of goma wheat served with *gomassio* (sesame seed and rock salt roasted together and pounded to a paste), oregano and olives. Some of the restaurant's ingredients are for sale.

Tex-Mex in Turkey

Bodrum is a surprising place to find good Tex-Mex food, but it is by no means impossible. If you are seeking an alternative to the standard tourist fayre, The Picante serves nachos and tacos for starters and very palate-pleasing tapas (eggplant and parmigiana slices, shrimps baked in artichoke with béchamel sauce) or the corn tortilla soup. *Fajitas* come in fish, meat and vegetarian form, and black-eyed chicken is another favourite.

Vejetaryen (£)

Chicken is available but this small, plain establishment, tucked away to the rear of the Hilton hotel, is still the nearest İzmir gets to a vegetarian restaurant. Simple dishes of spinach, beans and vegetarian kebabs. The fig dessert is worth trying.

✉ 1375 Sokak 11 ☎ (0232) 421 7558 🕑 8AM–8PM 🚌 62, 68, 77

Kuşadası

Bolu Mengen 11 (£)

A typical Kuşadası restaurant, but the claim to be open 24 hours sets it apart from the establishments further up this pedestrianised street in the heart of the town. Tables inside and out. As well as the main menu of grills and salads, there are also *lokanta*-style Turkish dishes to choose from (▶ 87).

✉ Sağlık Caddesi 56 ☎ (0256) 612 4114 🕑 24 hours

Club Cappello (££)

An appealing decor, with assorted artefacts hanging from the ceiling. Open wood fire for out-of-season chilly evenings, and outdoor tables for summer nights. Small menu, including fish at market prices and a wine list. Close to Korumar hotel, off the road to Selçuk.

✉ Akyar Mevki ☎ (0256) 614 4043 🕑 8:30–late 🚐 *Dolmuş*/minibus to Korumar hotel will stop outside

Doga (£)

A rustic-style interior and a pleasing absence of plastic furniture contribute to the pleasant atmosphere of this glorified café. The menu is in Turkish and English (same prices) and covers the gamut of light meals: breakfast, pizzas, omelettes, sandwiches. A good selection of teas.

✉ Adnan Menderes Bulvarı 1 ☎ (0256) 614 1039 🕑 8AM–9PM

Golden Pizzeria (£)

Small, modern, licensed café with a large menu of over 20 pizzas to choose from, and other possibilities, including English-style breakfast and a children's menu. A few doors up on the same side of the street, opposite the Otel Atadan, there is a less expensive, unlicensed *pide* (pizza) café specialising in the one dish: a tasty mixed *pide*, with or without meat, accompanied by a Turkish yogurt.

✉ Ismet Inönö Bulvarı 19 ☎ (0256) 614 5417 🕑 8–late

Güldüoğlu (££–£££)

In the centre of town, close to Beer Street, this is an elegant, air-conditioned restaurant with rosewood furniture and purchasable modern art by the painter/proprietor adorning the walls. Mixed menu – grills and pasta dishes – in English, Dutch, French, German and Spanish. Some tables outside.

✉ 1/C Zabita Amirliğ, Alti ☎ (0256) 614 8637 🕑 8am–11PM 🚐 Free transport to/from hotel

Holiday Inn (£)

In the heart of Kuşadası, and with a wide-ranging menu designed to appeal to overseas visitors: salads, lasagne, kebabs, moussaka, chicken kiev, roast beef, steaks, fish and chips, wiener schnitzel etc. Stick with the home-made kebabs and you won't be disappointed.

✉ Kahramanlar Caddesi 57/5 ☎ (0256) 612 8940 ⏰ 8AM–midnight 🚌 free transport

Sultan Han (£££)

A charming setting in the old part of town; the Sultan Han is in a renovated old caravanserai and some care has been taken to retain a traditional atmosphere. The menu is fairly wide-ranging but the Turkish dishes are the ones to go for. The *meze* are very tasty and there is a good selection of traditional, sugary, Turkish desserts. Belly dancers sometimes provide live entertainment.

✉ Bahar Sokak 8 ☎ (0256) 614 6380/614 3849 ⏰ Lunch and dinner

Selçuk

Özdamar (£)

The pedestrianised street that begins at the Artemis fountain has a number of almost identical restaurants: this is the one nearest to the fountain. A multilingual menu (English, Flemish, French, Italian and German) features mostly grills, pizzas and salads. Outdoor tables and long hours.

✉ Cengiz Topel Caddesi 65 ☎ (0232) 891 4097 ⏰ 7:30AM–midnight

Pink Bistro (£)

The menu includes hamburgers, spaghetti, kebabs, Turkish pizza and salads. It is not gourmet dining, but it is pleasant enough. Late at night this is a lively bar playing taped music to a European clientele in the 20–30 age group.

✉ Atatürk Mh Saigburg Sokak ☎ (0232) 891 4015 ⏰ 9AM–2:30PM

Seçkin (££)

The food is well presented and the service is unobtrusive in this terrace restaurant on the pedestrianised Çengiz Topel Caddesi.

✉ Çengiz Topel Caddesi ☎ (0232) 892 6698

Selçuk Köftecisi (£–££)

Do not be put off by the plain interior and lack of a menu. With a reputation among locals as the best place in town for *köfte* (meatballs), this place is worth finding behind the bank opposite the post office. Try the *köfte* with a salad and some kebabs, a glass of *raki* and a pudding to finish off.

✉ Vergi Dairesi altı 37/J ☎ (0232) 892 6696 ⏰ 7AM–midnight

Truva (Troy)

Helen (£)

Although Çanakkale is the best place for a meal (▶ 92) when you are visiting Troy, there are a few possibilities in the village of Trevfikiye, which is within walking distance of the site entrance. Of these the Helen is undoubtedly the best, serving tasty meals from a menu of Turkish and international favourites.

✉ Trevfikiye ☎ (0286) 283 1026 ⏰ Breakfast, lunch and dinner 🚌 *Dolmuş*/minibus to Çanakkale

Fresh Fish

Fresh fish caught locally is one of the delights of Turkey. The price may vary according to weight and the market. Sardines (*sardalya*), grey mullet (*kefal*) and black bream (*sangöz*) are usually the least expensive but it is worth spending more for bass (*levrek*), turbot (*kalkan*) and gilt-head bream (*çipura*).

Southern Aegean

Gender Rules
Once off the beaten tourist track, women travellers may find themselves being ushered into a separate room in a restaurant, or placed in a corner as far away from the male customers as possible. This is the way things are in Turkey and it would be considered very rude to create a fuss. In the resort areas, on the other hand, separation of the sexes has long been forgotten.

Bodrum

Ali Kaptan (££)
The chef has a reputation for preparing traditional European and Turkish favourites plus the occasional, more sophisticated special dish at this restaurant by the Eden Hotel.

✉ **Dr Mümtaz Ataman Caddesi** ☎ **(0252) 316 8686** 🕐 **Lunch and dinner**

Amphora (£–££)
Easy to find, opposite the marina, with tables outside on the pavement as well as inside this attractive old building. Turkish carpets add an Ottoman touch and the service is friendly. A well-established restaurant.

✉ **Neyzen Tevfik 164** ☎ **(0252) 316 2368** 🕐 **Lunch and dinner**

Buğay (££)
Highly recommended Turkish vegetarian cuisine at any time of the day. Meals are served outside in a small courtyard, or inside next to the shelves of wholefood produce and ingredients. Specials are on the blackboard; and be sure to try one of the herbal teas or the orchid root drink.

✉ **Türkuyusu Caddesi** ☎ **(0252) 316 2969** 🕐 **Mon–Sat, 8:30AM–11PM**

The Difference (££)
The Dutch chef and proprietor brings a touch of European *élan* to the menu. The home-made soups are tasty, and, the steaks are well above the usual standard.

✉ **Narrow street running from Atatürk Caddesi to the sea** ☎ **(0252) 316 8396** 🕐 **Lunch and dinner**

The Han (££)
The food is an unoriginal mixture of Turkish and international dishes, but the location is more unusual – the restaurant is in a renovated *han* – an Ottoman inn – and there is the bonus of live evening entertainment. Oriental dancers warm up the atmosphere, and customers who have drunk enough *raki* are tempted to try out a belly dance or two, to the accompaniment of drums and flutes.

✉ **Kale Sokak** ☎ **(0252) 316 7951/316 1615** 🕐 **Lunch and dinner**

Kocadon (£££)
This is the way one would like all of Bodrum to look; the restaurant is set among ancient-looking stone walls and houses enclosing a quiet courtyard with a small pool in a garden. Sparkling white linen on the tables, jazz or classical music in the background, and good Turkish cuisine add to the air of romance. Make a reservation and arrive in time to enjoy a cocktail by the poolside and soak up the atmosphere.

✉ **Neyzen Tevfik Caddesi 160** ☎ **(0252) 614 63705** 🕐 **8PM–midnight**

Cavallino (££)
An Italian-style restaurant in the Günden Resort hotel, at the west, Gümbet (Bitez), end of town. It overlooks the pool, and the excellent food tastes authentically Italian. There's also a good wine list.

✉ **Günden Resort Hotel, Gümbet** ☎ **(0252) 313 4382** 🕐 **Lunch and dinner** 🚌 *Dolmuş*/minibus to Bodrum

Kardeşler (£)

There are wooden tables inside, plastic tables outside and no air-conditioning. The menu features kebabs and fish dishes like octopus salad. Licensed and in the centre of town, it is suitable for a cheapish no-frills meal.

✉ Yeni Çarşı Akbank Bitişiği 10 ☎ (0252) 614 6228
🕐 8AM–11PM

Nur (££)

An elegant Mediterranean setting successfully evoked in the courtyard of a town house. The menu is not large and the portions are not huge, but there is a good selection of fish and meat dishes, and the atmosphere of the place compensates.

✉ Cumhuriyet Caddesi, Eski Adilye Sokak 5 ☎ (0252) 313 1065 🕐 Lunch and dinner

Picante (££–£££)

Tex-Mex food (► 94, panel) is served in this very popular and chic restaurant, not easy to find in one of the quieter corners of Bodrum (► 60). Make an evening of it and turn up well before your reservation for drinks at the little bar; the wine list includes imported wines. There are outdoor tables at the back.

✉ Türkkuyusu Mah Kğlcu Sokak 8 ☎ (0252) 316 0270
🕐 8AM–2:30PM

Sandal (££)

Established for over 10 years, the Thai-owned Sandal claims to be the first and only original Thai and Chinese restaurant in Turkey. The cooks are from Thailand and there is a fair choice of dishes from the à la carte menu. Fixed-priced lunch and dinner meals are also available. The restaurant is located at the Halikarnas disco end of town.

✉ Atatürk Caddesi 74 ☎ (0252) 316 9117 🕐 Lunch and dinner

Sunny's (££)

Just 500m from the Halikarnas Disco but very popular with visitors across Bodrum as a whole. The menu goes from the sublime – Turkish specialties like lamb with aubergine sauce – to the prosaic (British steak and kidney pie). Tucked away down a narrow street between the sea and Atatürk Caddesi.

✉ Cumhuriyet Caddesi, Rasathane Sokak 7 ☎ (0252) 316 5286 🕐 8AM–late

Datça

Liman (£–££)

One of the many restaurants overlooking the west cove. The quality and choice of food is reasonably similar at all of them, but the Liman has a terrace and is very popular.

✉ Seafront, Datça 🕐 Lunch and dinner 🚌 Bus to Marmaris; car and passenger ferry from Körmen, 9km north, to Bodrum

Fethiye & Ölüdeniz

Anfora (££)

One of the smarter-looking restaurants in Fethiye, with jazz photographs on the wall, stone walls and giant plants in pots. Serving Turkish and continental food, it's sometimes invaded by hotel groups, but usually a reasonably quiet place.

✉ Fethiye ☎ (0252) 612 1282
🕐 Lunch and dinner

Meze

Often translated as appetisers or hors d'oeuvres, Turkish *meze* are neither of those things. Vegetarians can make a full meal out of three or four on a plate accompanied with rice and bread. A full-scale Turkish meal starts with a selection of cold, then hot *meze* and by the time the main course arrives the appetite can be flagging. Especially filling are the green peppers stuffed with rice, nuts and currants, and cooked in olive oil.

Raki

The national alcoholic drink is distilled from grape juice and flavoured with aniseed. It is usually mixed with water, whereupon it becomes cloudy, and is drunk with meals. The high alcohol content, over 40 per cent, may explain why it is not so popular as an aperitif, because it certainly packs a punch on an empty stomach. Try it with some cheese and water-melon.

Günes (££)

Well-established, large tourist restaurant in the bazaar area of town, with tables inside and out. Try to avoid peak times, when tour groups turn up en masse. Hot and cold starters, meat and fish. No surprises.

✉ **Likya Sokak 4–5, Fethiye**
🕐 **Lunch and dinner**

Meğri (£)

A well-established restaurant that has acquired a good reputation for its authentic Turkish meals. To order, just point to the dish you want. There is a second Meğri restaurant in Çarşı Caddesi.

✉ **Eski Cami Gecidi Likya Sokak 8, Fethiye** ☎ **(0252) 614 4046** 🕐 **Lunch and dinner**

Restaurant La Turquoise (££)

A poolside hotel restaurant that serves international cuisine. The pleasant setting and the live classical Turkish music contribute to the ambience of fine dining.

✉ **Montana Pine Resort, Ölüdeniz** ☎ **(0252) 616 6366**
🕐 **Lunch and dinner**
🚌 **Dolmuş/minibus from Fethiye**

Sesa Park (£)

This is a reasonably good restaurant in a nondescript hotel. It has air-conditioning and is one of the few places where a decent meal can be enjoyed at this end of Fethiye, not too far from the Lycian rock tombs. The pizzas are worth trying, and there is a reasonable selection of other dishes.

✉ **Akdeniz Caddesi 17, Fethiye**
☎ **(0252) 614 4656**
🕐 **7:30AM–10PM**

Göcek

Göcek (£–££)

Göcek, on the main coastal road between Fethiye and Köyceğiz, attracts travellers passing through with their own transport, and also yachting customers, who tend to push the prices up a little. The fresh fish is tempting, though, and the surrounding landscape makes a peaceful setting.

✉ **Yat Club House** ☎ **(0252) 645 1414** 🕐 **Lunch and dinner**
🚌 **Dolmuş/minibus to Fethiye and Köyceğiz**

Gümüşlük

Akvaryom (££)

Restaurants do not come much closer to the sea than this one. Fresh fish is the specialty and the quality of the food, plus the ambience of the marine setting, makes the journey from Marmaris worthwhile.

✉ **Seafront** ☎ **(0252) 394 3682** 🕐 **Lunch and dinner**
🚌 **Dolmuş/minibus from Bodrum**

İçmeler

Deefne (££)

The fixed-priced buffet in this hotel restaurant features a reasonable selection of *meze* and continental dishes, and you eat to the accompaniment of live classical music. The water *dolmuş* from Marmaris stops at the back of the hotel. English and German spoken.

✉ **Munumar Hotel, Keykubat Caddesi** ☎ **(0252) 455 3359**
🕐 **7PM–9:30PM**
🚌 **Dolmuş/minibus and water dolmuş from Marmaris**

Marmaris

Alba (££–£££)
A relatively new restaurant in Marmaris, but already well spoken of and gaining a reputation as an exclusive establishment. The hilltop location has no small part to play – but the European cuisine can hold its own.
✉ Kaleiçi 30, Sokak 10
☎ (0252) 412 4299 🕐 Lunch and dinner

Antique (££–£££)
The location, on the first-floor balcony of the Nestel Marina, gives the Antique an edge over restaurants with lesser views. All are welcome, and the food is excellent, especially the salads.
✉ Nestel Marina ☎ (0252) 412 2708 🕐 8AM–late

Dede (££)
The Dede is near the tourist office. The vast menu, in English, German and Russian, includes *meze*, steaks, chicken, kebabs and seafood. Indoor and outdoor tables.
✉ Barbaros Caddesi 15
☎ (0252) 413 1289
🕐 8am–midnight

Mr Zek (££)
A popular restaurant with live music and a relaxed atmosphere. The food is a cut above the average and includes soups, fish and meat main courses, and a good selection of European and Turkish desserts.
✉ Harbour front ☎ (0252) 413 4123 🕐 Lunch and dinner

Mona Titti (££)
The brightly coloured exterior is easy to spot on the waterfront. The menu is imaginative and the curries are some of the best you are likely to enjoy on the coast.
✉ Atatürk Caddesi ☎ (0252) 412 8799 🕐 Lunch and dinner

Pineapple (££)
Another restaurant in the Nestel Marina, this one is on the ground floor, and residents of Marmaris rate it as one of the best half dozen in the town. International cuisine, in a pastoral setting.
✉ Nestel Marina ☎ (0252) 412 0976 🕐 8AM–late

Rovers Return (£)
In a pleasant garden setting near the sea. Suitable for families with young children who like sausage and chips, omelettes and other favourites of that sort.
✉ Behind the Atlas Hotel, Kemel El 🕐 8AM–9PM

Türkbükü

Mey (££)
It floats on a platform in the sea, and fish is the speciality. Not the only restaurant of its kind in Türkbükü but it is a popular one.
✉ Türkbükü, northern coast of Bodrum peninsula ☎ (0252) 377 5118 🕐 Lunch and dinner
🚌 *Dolmuş*/minibus to Marmaris

Yalıkavak

Ali Baba (££)
Overlooking the harbour, this is an ideal spot to enjoy home-made *meze*, with fish and steaks for a main course. *Pide* bread is cooked here in a traditional oven.
✉ Seafront ☎ (0252) 385 4063 🕐 Lunch and dinner
🚌 *Dolmuş*/minibus from Bodrum

Pastries and Puddings
Pastry shops are *pastahanes*. For sheer sugary, gooey indulgence there is nothing to beat a typical Turkish pastry, soaked in rich oil and filled with cream or syrup. Turkish puddings are just as sweet and also pose a challenge to anyone watching their weight. The most famous sweet, Turkish delight (*lokum*), is made from solidified sugar and pectin, usually flavoured with rosewater and sprinkled with icing sugar.

Northern Aegean

Prices

Approximate prices per room per night, regardless of single or double occupancy. Because the lira is so unstable, the categories are given in US dollars.

£ = US$20–40
££ = US$40–60
£££ = over US$60

Çanakkale

Akol (££–£££)

This 4-star hotel at the east end of town is the most comfortable accommodation base for visits to Troy and Gallipoli. The two blocks have a small pool in between. About 75 per cent of the 136 rooms face the Dardanelles, and there are two restaurants and a roof bar.

✉ **Kordonboyu** ☎ **(0286) 217 9456; fax (0286) 217 2897**

Anzac House (£)

A good choice for budget accommodation in Çanakkale. The hostel-style dormitory rooms are clean, and facilities include a cafeteria downstairs serving inexpensive meals, a laundry service, and hot water showers. This is also a centre for booking Troy and Gallipoli tours, and films about Gallipoli are shown in the evening. Centrally located, on the left about 500m before the main docking area for ferries across the Dardanelles. Open all year.

✉ **Cumhuriyet Meydanı 61** ☎ **(0286) 217 1392; fax (0286) 217 2906**

Herakleia

Agora (£)

This is one of the most pleasant places for an overnight stay amidst the evocative remains of ancient Herakleia (the modern village name is Kapıkırı). Simple pine beds, a pleasant veranda and lots of local information. No English but German is spoken, and local trekking trips are arranged with a guide.

✉ **Kapıkırı** ☎ **(0252) 543 5445; fax (0252) 543 5567**
🚍 **Dolmuş/minibus from Çamiçi or by boat from southern shore of Lake Bafa**

Zeybek (£)

A less expensive alternative to the Agora and worth considering if staying only one night in Herakleia. Local information is available, no English but some German is spoken.

✉ **Kapıkırı**
🚍 **Dolmuş/minibus from Çamiçi or by boat from southern shore of Lake Bafa**

İzmir

Büyük Efes (£££)

This is one of the best hotels on the Aegean coast, with a distinctive interior styling that makes clever use of greenery and traditional Turkish designs. A disco, nightclub and Turkish bath make it popular with non-residents. Excellent restaurants.

✉ **Gaziosmanpasa Bulvarı** ☎ **(0232) 484 4300; fax: (0232) 441 5695** 🚍 **61–63, 116, 110, 112, 150**

Hilton (£££)

The 34 storeys make this the tallest building on the Aegean coast. Good sports centre, pool, disco, excellent restaurants and a bar on the 31st floor with a terrific view. Standard of service as high as one would expect from a Hilton. Airport shuttle bus stops nearby.

✉ **Gaziosmanpasa Bulvarı** ☎ **(0232) 441 6060; fax (0232) 441 2277; e-mail izmhitw@hilton.com** 🚍 **61–63, 116, 110, 112, 150**

Imperial (£)

Probably the best accommodation available for this price category in İzmir. Small, but the rooms are clean and have their own toilet and shower. There is a lot of Turkish character to the place. Preferable by far to the other budget places in this part of town (near the main railway station).

✉ 1296 Sokak 54, Basmane
☎ (0232) 484 9771; fax (0232) 425 6883 🚌 153

Princess (£££)

Well outside the town centre in Balçova, but easily reached by taxi or bus, and the hotel has its own free shuttle service. The compensation for the time spent travelling is a health centre that uses the local thermal water. It even comes out of the bath taps.

✉ Balçova ☎ (0232) 238 5151; fax (0232) 239 0939 🚌 109

Kuşadası

Derici (££)

On the beachfront in the centre of town. Each of the 87 rooms has a balcony, and about one third offer sea views. Unusually there is a swimming pool on the 7th floor, alongside a bar with a sweeping view of the Aegean.

✉ Atatürk Bulvarı 40
☎ (0256) 614 8222; fax (0256) 614 8226

Grand Blue Sky (£££)

A five-star hotel at the Ladies' Beach end of town. All the rooms have balconies and seaviews. There is a small, private beach with a diving school and water sports. There are also indoor and outdoor restaurants, a fitness centre, sauna and Turkish bath.

✉ Kadınlar Denizli ☎ (0256) 612 7750; fax (0256) 612 4225
🚌 Dolmuş/minibus to Kuşadası town centre

Korumar (£££)

Just off the road heading out of town towards Selçuk, this five-star, 250-room hotel looks out across the Aegean. There are outdoor and indoor pools, three restaurants, an open-air disco, Turkish bath, sauna and solarium. Open all year.

✉ Off road to Selçuk ☎ (0256) 614 8243; fax (0256) 614 5596 🚌 Dolmuş/minibus to Kuşadası town centre

Selçuk

Kalehan (££)

The Ottoman charm of the Kalehan puts it in a class of its own. Within walking distance of Efes (Ephesus), on the main road through town, the rooms are delightfully furnished and comfortably modern as well. Antiques and artefacts are everywhere and lend character to the place. There is a swimming pool and good restaurant.

✉ Atatürk Caddesi 4a
☎ (0232) 892 6154; fax (0232) 892 2169

Nazhan (£)

This is the best pansiyon in Selçuk. There are six tastefully furnished rooms (four en suite), and the tariff includes breakfast in the tiny courtyard. The roof bar is attractive and meals are cooked on request.

✉ Saint Jean Caddesi, 1044 Sokak ☎ (0232) 892 8731

Looking for a Room

If you are travelling around you should be able to find rooms on the spot, except in the more popular resorts of Kuşadası, Bodrum and Marmaris. In these places it is best to ask the tourist office for help. If travelling by public transport in summer, you are likely to be approached by touts at the station, but, unless you are desperate you should reject their offers of help. They can be unreliable, and will expect a commission from the proprietor, who will add it to your bill.

Southern Aegean

Pansiyons

For an inexpensive night's lodging, look for a *pansiyon* (pension) sign. A *pansiyon* is a cross between a bed and breakfast and a small guesthouse, and is typically a friendly and welcoming place. Rooms tend to be plain but clean and the better ones will have their own toilet and shower. Hot water and some kind of laundry facility is usually provided, and breakfast is always available, but may cost extra.

Bergama/Pamukkale

Kervansaray (£–££)

There is nowhere particularly attractive to stay in Bergama itself and the motels up on the Pamukkale plateau tend to be expensive, but this well-established place in the small village between the two is well run, clean and friendly. There is a restaurant on the roof and the rooms have their own showers.

İnönü Caddesi, Pamukkale Köyü ☎ (0258) 272 2209; fax (0258) 272 2143 Taxi from Bergama

Koray Otel (£–££)

Budget travellers speak well of this place. It is quiet and welcoming, there is a little garden and meals are cooked on request.

Off Menderes Caddesi, Pamukkale Köyü ☎ (0258) 272 2222; fax (0258) 272 2095 taxi from Bergama

Bodrum

Durak (£)

This is a relatively quiet little *pansiyon*, notwithstanding its position at the Halikarnas disco end of town. A neat little front garden and terrace adds to the charm of the place. All rooms have their own toilet and shower and some also have a small balcony. The Uğur (☎ (0252) 3162106), next door, is also worth trying if Durak is full.

Rasathane Sokak 8 ☎ (0252) 316 1564

Emiko (£)

This is another charming little *pansiyon*, in a central position in town but not too noisy at night. It represents fairly good value, especially since all the rooms are en suite with their own toilet and shower.

Atatürk Caddesi, Uslu Sok 11 ☎ (0252) 316 5560

Karia Princess (£££)

This award-winning hotel is the classiest place to stay in the whole of Bodrum. It is a little way to the west of the town centre and consequently not plagued by disco music at 3AM. There is, however, a neat little cinema near by and the largest supermarket to be found in any of the resort towns along the coast. The hotel's Turkish bath is a superb recreation of an Ottoman-style *hamam*. Most rooms have a pleasant balcony, and the 20 per cent that don't are cheaper.

Canli Dere Sokak 15 ☎ (0252) 316 8971; fax (0252) 316 8979

Fethiye & Ölüdeniz

Anita and Ned's (£)

All the rooms here have their own bathrooms and can be booked on a bed and breakfast, half-board, full-board or self-catering basis. Some distance from Fethiye but a wonderfully quiet location, surrounded by pine forests and with a small beach about 3km away and Calis beach within an hour's walk. Home-cooked meals are available and vegetarians are catered for. Anita and Ned's is not for those who want a sun and sand holiday, but a good place to 'get away from it all'.

Ciftlikkoy, 12km from Fethiye ☎ (0252) 623 9783 *Dolmuş*/minibus to Fethiye

Kemal (££)

The Kemal is in the very centre of town, behind the post office and with en-suite rooms, simply but pleasantly furnished, facing the sea. Away from the pubs and comfortably quiet at night. Open all year.

✉ **Kordon Boyu Gezi Yolu, Fethiye** ☎ (0252) 614 5009; fax (0252) 614 5009

Meri (£££)

This is the place to soak up the sun at Ölüdeniz, and the only hotel inside the designated national park area. There are 75 rooms, a restaurant and garden bar, a playground area for children and laundry. All the usual water-based activities can be arranged here, including diving.

✉ **Ölüdeniz** ☎ (0252) 616 6060; fax (0252) 616 6456
🚌 *Dolmuş*/minibus to Fethiye

İçmeler

Aqua (£££)

Pleasantly landscaped, with palm trees and a garden leading down to the beach. The amenities of İçmeler are within walking distance. The 240 rooms have balconies with partial sea views. Suitable for families with children; adults can use the fitness centre, gym and tennis court.

✉ **İçmeler** ☎ (0252) 455 3633; fax (0252) 455 3650
🚌 *Dolmuş*/minibus to Marmaris

Munamar Vista (£££)

About half of the rooms have a sea view. The hotel itself backs on to the beach; and the water *dolmuş* from Marmaris makes its final stop here. Turkish bath, pool, fitness centre, disco, and large rooms; watersports gear for hire. Open all year.

✉ **Kayabal Caddesi** ☎ (0252) 455 3360; fax (0252) 455 3359
🚌 *Dolmuş*/minibus and water *dolmuş*, from Marmaris

Marmaris

Begonya (££)

This is a cut above the average mid-range hotel in the middle of Marmaris. It is a stone-built house with its own courtyard and become characterful architecture. The only disadvantage is the possibility of being kept awake by the nearby pubs.

✉ **Hacı Mustafa Sokak 101** ☎ (0252) 412 4095; fax (0252) 412 1518

Green Nature (£££)

This modern, five-star hotel, is popular with British tour operators. There is a swimming pool, with a children's pool and jacuzzi, buffet restaurant, sauna, fitness centre, Turkish and Finnish baths, tennis court and billiards.

✉ **Siteler Mh Armutalan** ☎ (0252) 413 6054; fax (0252) 413 6052 🚌 *Dolmuş*/minibus to Marmaris

Kaya Maris (££)

Used by some British tour operators, this is a 256-room tourist hotel just 50m from the beach and a half-hour walk from central Marmaris. There is a main swimming pool and a children's pool, Turkish bath, gym, sauna, and water sports.

✉ **Kenan Evren Bulvarı** ☎ (0252) 413 0233; fax (0252) 413 1864 🚌 *Dolmuş*/minibus to Marmaris

Resort Hotels

Independent travellers can use the four- and five-star resort hotels, but they are far better value if booked as part of a package deal with a tour operator in your own country. Places are usually offered on a bed and breakfast or half-board basis. Families may prefer self-catering, and some of the big resort hotels provide this option. When meals are provided, they are invariably buffets and can become monotonous. Hotels charge extra for drinks at dinner, and some will do so even for a glass of water.

Bazaars

Carpets

Turkish carpets have an international reputation, but there are many differences in quality. Whether a carpet is handwoven or machine-made is fundamental to its value; other things that matter are the density of the knots in handwoven carpets, whether the dyes are either natural or less expensive chemical ones, and whether the carpet is made of wools or silk. The flat-woven, double-sided mats known as *kilims* are always less expensive.

Kuşadası, Bodrum and Marmaris

The big resort towns of Kuşadası, Bodrum and Marmaris all have bazaars (*basar* in Turkish). They are not really the genuine Ottoman emporia that still survive in their medieval forms in Istanbul, and to a lesser extent in İzmir. They are still great places to shop, however, and are based around the traditional shopping areas of town.

Resort bazaars consist of small shops on either side of a pedestrianised street or passageway, many with awnings over their street displays of merchandise. The advantage for the consumer is a high density of tourist-oriented shops, all competing with one another, and the cool shade of the awnings is welcome relief in the high season. The drawback is that the constant importuning by proprietors and roaming touts can become tiresome, especially when you just want to be left alone to consider a purchase. The sales line usually begins with an offer of tea, but bear in mind that such hospitality comes naturally to Turkish people and no commitment is being sought when the offer is made.

The merchandise covers a wide range, especially in Marmaris where boat loads of visitors from Greece arrive daily with Turkish money to spend. Shops selling leather clothing and goods – handbags, travel bags, briefcases, accessories – are all over the place, closely followed by stores selling carpets and *kilims*, jewellery,

meerschaum pipes, ceramics and crafts.

It is worth checking out some of the clothes stores with familiar branded North American and European labels, for these are usually made under licence in Turkey and are consequently often much less expensive than back home. You should check the quality, however. The least expensive items in a bazaar will usually be souvenirs, synthetic apple tea powder, sandals and beachwear, Turkish delight (*lokum*) and other sweets.

İzmir

The maze of narrow streets and cul-de-sacs to the north of Konak Square that make up the city's bazaar date from before the fire of 1922 (► 31). There are a number of restored 18th century caravanserai (where the trading caravans from the East would rest) and a few mosques, including the Hisar Mosque from 1597. This is both the oldest and the largest mosque in İzmir. The bazaar is a place where it is easy to get lost (see the guided walk, ► 33).

The countless shops, stalls and workshops are used by Turks rather than tourists, and the clothes and shoe shops are well worth looking into, as are the music shops where the traditional folk music scene flourishes. The atmosphere is the main attraction: it is a place of great interest and character and is still the best place to immerse yourself in the sounds, sights and smells of Turkish culture. Avoid going on Sundays, when most of the shops are closed.

Traditional Crafts & Souvenirs

Antiques

Northern Aegean

Bergama

Tahsin Bayansal
A large shop full of old bronze, copper and wooden utensils that once served a practical purpose. Silver items are also on sale, as are embroidered cloth, glass, and old carpets and *kilims*. Serious bargaining is in order because this shop, located opposite the Red Basilica, is aimed squarely at visitors to Pergamum, and opening prices are pitched way above the real value.

✉ **Kinik Caddesi 9** ☎ **(0232) 633 1974** 🕐 **9AM–11PM**

Bodrum

Ifos
There are two floors, the upper level devoted to old kilims and small carpets, the ground floor crammed full with a miscellany of objects. Not everything is a genuine antique, nor is it claimed to be, and there is a lot to see: this is a good shop to look around when you are not in a hurry. The collection of hookahs, old and contemporary, is one of the highlights.

✉ **Çarşi Mahallesı Çarşi İçı 6, Sokak 16** ☎ **(0252) 316 4961** 🕐 **9AM–midnight**

Southern Aegean

Marmaris

Ottoman
A miscellany of silver jewellery, clocks, pocket watches, copper utensils of all shapes and sizes, hand embroidery and other items. Part of the pleasure of this shop is its air of disorder, with widely assorted goods in a chaotic-looking arrangement. It is a serious shop, though with many genuine antiques, and shipping can be arranged. Inland, near the bazaar.

✉ **Çeşme Mey Grand Pazar 1** ☎ **(0252) 412 5911** 🕐 **9AM–10PM**

Arts & Crafts

Northern Aegean

Çanakkale

Ilion Tur
One branch of this store is just outside Troy in the village of Trevfikiye, but the Çanakkale shop is a better one to visit as it is not subject to invasion by tour bus crowds. There is the usual Troy memorabilia here, but this is the least expensive place. Also on sale are Turkish baggy pants, books on ancient history and assorted souvenirs. The stalls facing the main vehicle ferry dock in the town centre sell the cheapest Troy souvenirs.

✉ **Yali Caddesi 20** ☎ **(0286) 217 0537 (**☎ **(0286) 283 0823 at Troy)** 🕐 **9AM–11PM**

Çeşme

Erdal's
Small gifts and souvenirs: crystal, ceramics, brass and copper, onyx, wood carvings, meerschaum pipes.

✉ **16 Eylül Mh Gümrük Caddesi 21** ☎ **(0232) 712 6161** 🕐 **8:30–9** 🚌 *Dolmuş*/minibus to İzmir

The Evil Eye

The belief that some people are capable of inflicting mental and physical harm through their 'evil eye' has a long history in Turkish culture (▶ 32). The antidote comes in the form of blue beads attached to pendants, chains and even key-rings. Jewellery shops sell the best-quality versions.

Negotiating Skills
Fixed and marked prices are a rarity along the Turkish Aegean, and some haggling is inevitable. Use your experience and judgement to assess what you are prepared to pay and try to compare prices between stores. As a general rule avoid making an offer (which you can never reduce) until the seller has made at least one reduction on their opening price.

Kuşadası

Asia Shop 2
Tucked away in a street to the rear of Grand Bazaar and best reached by walking up the street behind the tourist office, this store is worth seeking out if you need to buy a lot of small gifts and souvenirs. There are two floors crammed with inexpensive bric-à-brac, and the fixed prices mean you can wander around looking and choosing instead of having to haggle.
- ⊠ **Kibris Caddesi 4** ☎ **(0256) 614 1393** ⏱ **7:30–1AM**

Çerge
This is one of the more tasteful little shops in Kuşadası, partly because it is not totally dependent on tourist trade. In the winter, Turkish shoppers come here to buy attractive decorative items for their homes, while in summer the shop appeals to visitors looking for something more than a cheap souvenir.
- ⊠ **Kemal Ankan Caddesi 16**
- ☎ **(0256) 612 5821**
- ⏱ **8:30–midnight**

Music Box
A fair selection of cassettes and CDs, but the real attraction here is the traditional Turkish musical instruments for sale. There are simple flutes (*ney*) that are easy to carry, as well as larger and more delicate instruments.
- ⊠ **Yıldırım Caddesi 13**
- ☎ **(0256) 614 7522** ⏱ **9–1AM**

Pearl
A mixed collection of elegant Turkish arts and crafts, mostly modern in style and consisting of items such as decorative swords, clocks and jewellery. There are also some paintings framed in boxes, with a three-dimensional effect achieved by the layering of material on the small canvas.
- ⊠ **Kemal Arikan Caddesi 2**
- ☎ **(0256) 612 0553**
- ⏱ **10AM–11PM**

Priene

Onyx Factory & Shop
The workshop and adjoining store are in the corner of the square where the minibuses arrive and depart. Unless the shop is very busy, someone is usually glad to show you around the workshop and explain the process, from the arrival of the uncut stone to its final polishing. Prices are reasonable, and there is a good selection.
- ⊠ **Priene** ☎ **(0256) 547 1123**
- ⏱ **8AM–9PM**
- 🚌 *Dolmuş*/minibus from Söke

Southern Aegean

Didim (Didyma)/ Altınkum

Gallery Kirşehir
An onyx factory and shop, directly opposite the temple of Apollo, with vases, jars, ashtrays and other assorted items. Potential customers are shown around the factory.
- ⊠ **Harabeler Kar, Didyma**
- ☎ **(0256) 811 0306**
- ⏱ **8AM–9PM**
- 🚌 *Dolmuş*/minibus from Söke

Marmaris

Blue and White
Ceramic pieces made in Kütahya in the 18th century

are now prize exhibits in museums around the world. The town is still the centre of production for contemporary Turkish ceramics and there is a reasonable selection of them in this shop. The stock has been chosen with tourists in mind, which means that it's colourful, and they supply bubble wrapping and boxes to help you get the goods home safely. Prices are sensible too. In the centre of town, opposite the old mosque.

🖂 **Eski Camci Sok 57/A**
☎ **(0252) 412 0748**
🕒 **9AM–midnight**

Continental

Sells only Turkish ceramics, mostly plates and vases. Some of the hand-painted work is beautiful, and packaging is provided. Easy to find, in the bazaar.

🖂 **Eski Carsi Sokak 28/A**
☎ **(0252) 413 4008**
🕒 **9AM–midnight**

Nur-Bal

A jar or two of Marmaris honey is a distinctive local souvenir, and this little shop, in the block behind the post office, has a good selection. The dark-coloured, black-pine honey is one of the local specialties but also ask to see some *portakal*, a light-coloured and very sweet variation.

🖂 **Fevzi Paça Caddesi 9/C**
🕒 **8:30AM–10PM**

Carpets

Northern Aegean

İzmir

Anatolia

High-quality handwoven carpets and *kilims* are sold here. The selection is not huge but broad enough for anyone seriously thinking of making a purchase. For smaller purchases, expect a discount of at least 15 per cent. For really expensive carpets at least 25 per cent should be taken off the asking price.

🖂 **928 Sokak 25 (Hilton Hotel Shopping Mall)** ☎ **(0232) 441 7578** 🕒 **Mon–Sat 9–9**
🚌 **61–63, 116, 110, 112, 150**

Mihrap

Handwoven carpets of silk, wool and cotton and a selection of *kilims*. Bargain hard and expect at least 30 per cent off the asking price. Tucked away in a modern little mall in the bazaar. Look for the Parfümerai shop on a corner along Anafartalar Caddesi – the entrance to the mall is alongside it.

🖂 **Kapalicarsi, Anafartalar Caddesi, Konak** ☎ **(0232) 484 0425** 🕒 **9AM–7PM** 🚌 **86, 169**

Kuşadası

Faberce

This well-established store, easy to find near the entrance to the bazaar, opens early in the morning to catch passengers disembarking from the countless cruise ships that pause in Kuşadası. There are two floors of carpets and *kilims*, and the courteous staff don't go in for the hard sell – they are quite persuasive though. Delivery and insurance is arranged for bulky purchases, and this usually works out at around 2 per cent of the price.

🖂 **Söförler Sokak 3, Grand Bazaar** ☎ **(0256) 614 8885**
🕒 **7:30AM–midnight**

Long Hours

Unless otherwise stated, all the shops mentioned here are open seven days a week and never close for lunch. Typical hours are from 8 in the morning to 9 or 10 at night. In the popular resorts such as Kuşadası sales staff will still be asking you what country you come from and offering apple tea at well past midnight.

What to Buy?

Apart from the obvious, and more expensive, possibilities – leather, jewellery, carpets and ceramics – consider some of the less heavily touted items available along the coast. Wooden chess boards inlaid with cedar, or heavier onyx ones, are often of good value, as are portable backgammon (*tavla*) sets. Hookahs (*nargiles*) are ornamental; bowls and vases of alabaster are also worth looking out for.

Selçuk

Nomadic Art Gallery

Expensive, hand-woven wool carpets from Anatolia, less expensive cotton ones and also imports from Iran and Afghanistan. Customers will receive the usual cup of tea and lots of friendly conversation, but in any Selçuk carpet shop it pays to know something about carpets and to be able to distinguish between materials of different quality.

✉ **Atatürk Mh Cengiz Topel Caddesi 26/A** ☎ **(0232) 891 8650** 🕐 **8AM–11PM**

Southern Aegean

Bodrum

Galeri Anatolia

These two well-established stores claim to have the largest selection of Turkish carpets and *kilims* in Bodrum: a good place to start looking.

✉ **Kale Caddesi 2, Iskele Caddesi 11** ☎ **(0252) 614 62468, (0252) 614 61585** 🕐 **8AM–late**

Marmaris

Oriental

A self-styled 'carpet palace', this comfortable shop is easy to find, just next to the tourist office facing the sea. It has a reasonable selection of carpets and *kilims*, but you should go knowing something about what you want and the likely price – as in all such stores, the prices are not exactly the same for all customers. Some astute bargaining would not go amiss here.

✉ **Yat Limanı 3** ☎ **(0252) 412 4818** 🕐 **8AM–midnight**

Jewellery

Northern Aegean

İzmir

Sevgi Youlu

This is not a shop but a pedestrianised street directly behind the Hilton hotel. At weekends especially, the street is lined on both sides with stalls displaying trays of rings, pendants, chains and earrings. There are no marked prices but this is not a tourist market and prices, arrived at after weighing the merchandise, are very reasonable. Ask for a discount, and expect 10–20 per cent off the asking price.

✉ **Sevgi Youlu** 🕐 **9–9** 🚌 **62, 68, 77**

Selçuk

İahin

In the middle of Selçuk, close to the Artemis statue and on the corner of the pedestrianized street opposite the line of restaurants. Deals only in gold jewellery. Some English is spoken.

✉ **Namik Kemal Caddesi 2** ☎ **(0232) 891 8838** 🕐 **9AM–10PM**

Southern Aegean

Bodrum

Patika

Seek out this small shop, if only to admire the skill that has gone into sculpting the exquisite turquoise figurines for sale here. Other precious stones, such as opal, are also available, and there are modern-style rings, earrings and necklaces, in addition to the usual Ottoman-style jewellery and some attractive amber as well. Easy to find, on the right side of the main road that leads up from the mosque near the tourist office to the bus station (► 60).

✉ **Cevat Sakir Caddesi 18/A**
☎ **(0252) 313 2607**
🕓 **8:30AM–midnight**

Fethiye

Talisman
Shopping in Fethiye is limited, but this little store has one of the better selections of gold, silver and precious stones: mostly necklaces, rings, bangles and ornate earrings, none of them terribly expensive. Also does repairs.

✉ **Hamam Sokak 15/1**
☎ **(0252) 614 8585**
🕓 **9AM–7PM**

Southern Aegean

Kuşadası

Barok
A serious jewellery store, dealing in gold and precious stones only. Prices should be negotiated. In a central spot, opposite the main harbour.

✉ **C Kebir Mah Barbaros Caddesi 13** ☎ **(0256) 612 8098**
🕓 **9AM–11PM**

Leather

Northern Aegean

İzmir

Aydın
A good place for jackets, and not aimed specifically at the overseas tourist market. There are other competing leather stores near by, so it

might pay to look around and compare prices.

✉ **Gazi Osmanpaşa Bulvarı**
☎ **(0232) 489 2235** 🕓 **8–8**
🚌 **88, 92, 93, 157, 235**

Kuşadası

Galeri Sultan
Claims to be the oldest leather emporium in Kuşadası. A good collection of jackets and some less expensive waistcoats. A family-run shop with a prime location in the Grand Bazaar.

✉ **Grand Bazaar 5** ☎ **(0256) 612 4569** 🕓 **7:30AM–1AM**

Southern Aegean

Bodrum

Gazelle Leather & Gift Shop Handicraft
With a bit of a mixture of merchandise, there is a small collection of leather jackets and belts and a whole host of less expensive craft items, such as small inlaid boxes. There are also picture frames, a jewellery section, souvenirs and gifts.

✉ **Neyzen Tefik Caddesi 124**
☎ **(0252) 316 9707**
🕓 **9:30AM–midnight**

Marmaris

Duygu Bag Shop
A bazaar shop with quality leather travel bags, hand bags, belts and briefcases. There are marked prices on the items but you can still ask for a discount. There is a similar shop at the other end of the pedestrianised passageway, so compare products and prices.

✉ **Tepe Mah Rıhtım Sokak 11/A** ☎ **(0252) 412 8117**
🕓 **9AM–midnight**

Leather Jackets
Do not expect any great bargains: good Turkish leather jackets are not cheap, but they should be still cheaper than jackets of similar quality back home. Spend some time comparing prices and take time trying them on. Check the stitching carefully and be sure to take the jacket out of the shop to check the colour in natural light.

Children's Attractions

Babysitting in Bodrum

Gündüz Bakim Evi is a day care centre (✉ Umurça Mah Derviş Görgü Caddesi 12/2. ☎ (0252) 66328) for 3–6 year-olds, providing classes, meals and a playground. Babysitting is also available. English, French and German spoken.

Turkey does not have many attractions specifically designed for children, but it is a welcoming place for them all the same. Turks are usually quite happy to see children at shops and restaurants, and someone will always help with the pushchair in awkward places. You can get disposable nappies for babies up to 12kg at pharmacies, which also stock formula milk and baby food.

Most of the better resort hotels will have a children's pool separate from the main pool. Some hotels, usually in co-operation with a tour operator in your own country, have special clubs for children (3–6 year-olds and 7–12 year-olds) – effectively taking them off your hands for morning and afternoon sessions. Babysitting in the evening is not very easy to arrange.

Beaches

Western Turkey has plenty of beaches for young children who are happy to build sandcastles and play under supervision in shallow water. It can sometimes be difficult to find shady places on the sand, though, so remember hats, sunblock and other protection from the sun. Always check with your hotel and the tourist office about the advisability of swimming off the local beach: don't assume that just because parasols and deckchairs line the sand the sea must be safe. Apart from undertows and difficult currents, some stretches of sea are sometimes just too polluted to be healthy. The

beaches at Calis (➤ 64) and Turgetreis (➤ 89) are safe in so far as the sea there is shallow for a long way out. This is also true of the beach at İztuzu (Dalyan ➤ 65), which is a nesting site for loggerhead turtles.

Parks

Kültürpark

This is the main park in İzmir and is home to a zoo and amusement park as well as a restaurant and quiet gardens. It is also the site of the İzmir International Fair, but for most of the year it's a welcome oasis in the centre of the city.

Go-Karting

Go-Kart Club

Targeted at the visitor as well as the local Turkish market, it might be worth making a phone call to see what is on.
✉ Tepe Mah, Bağiç Sokak, Malakent Yanı, Marmaris
☎ (0252) 413 8958

Waterparks

Atlantis Aquapark & Aquapark İçmeler

The Atlantis Aquapark is a water-based fun park for children. It boasts a wide range of water slides and a 'froggy island'. There is a bar for parents. Aquapark İçmeler, under the same management as Atlantis is on the right as you enter İçmeler from Marmaris.
Atlantis Aquapark
✉ Marmaris ☎ (0252) 413 0308 ⏰ morning to evening
Aquapark İçmeler
☎ (0252) 455 5049 ⏰ morning to evening

Activities

Cinema (► panel)

Karia Princess Cinema

This is the neatest little cinema on the Turkish Aegean coast. It's in the bottom floor of a hotel in Bodrum,and has a small bar serving drinks and sweets. Come the obligatory intermission everyone still rushes out for a cigarette. Curious but cute.

✉ **Canli Dere Sokak 15, Bodrum** ☎ **(0252) 316 6272**
🕐 **Afternoon, evening and night shows**

Kuşadası Cinema

Most people will enjoy the spectacle of Kuşadası's outdoor cinema (indoor in winter) in the very centre of town. It is small and quaint and the sound of traffic does not prove a problem. Inexpensive as well.

✉ **Kemai Ankan Caddesi, Kuşadası** ☎ **(0256) 614 1370**
🕐 **Afternoon, evening and night shows**

Horse riding

Horse Safari & Horse Camp

A way for older children and adults to see the landscape from a different point of view. Bodrum's Horse Camp offers individual riding lessons, 1–2 hour trips and overnight trekking.

Hills Tour ✉ **Atatürk Bulvarı 70, Kuşadası.** ☎ **(0256) 612 8332**
Horse Camp ✉ **Bitez Beach** ☎ **(0252) 614 31961**

Walking

Although most of the serious walking in Turkey is done in the central mountains, this can still be a rewarding activity in the coastal regions, providing a glimpse of older, more traditional ways of life, away from the bustle of the resorts and tourist sites. Unfortunately, mapping is poor, so navigation can be difficult. Be wary of the heat and the sun, especially during the middle of the day. Wear a hat and carry plenty of water.

Saklıkent

This 18km-long gorge, so narrow in places that the sun doesn't reach it, makes an appealing day out for more experienced walkers. A wooden boardwalk takes you some of the way, but the walk also involves a little wading and scrambling. Bring a picnic, although there are places to eat should you want them.

✉ **Saklıkent, 46km southeast of Fethiye** 🕐 **8AM–5PM**
🚌 **Dolmuş/minibus to Fethiye**

Watersports and Adventure Tours

Windsurfing, parasailing, jet-skiing and canoeing (► 114) are the most popular activities, and snorkelling, under supervision, is enthralling for children.It's wise to check what your travel insurance says about accidents caused by watersports.

In the bigger resorts it is worth asking whether the agencies that handle boat trips can also arrange activities such as trekking, canoeing, or rafting. Older children are usually accepted, providing they have an adult with them. Try Natur Travel Agency ☎ (0252) 614 8994; fax (0252) 614 6992 or at their office in Olüdeniz ☎ (0252) 616 6586.

Films

Films originally in English are not usually dubbed, only subtitled in Turkish, and most of the big releases find their way into Turkish cinemas.

Pubs, Clubs, Discos & Bars

The Kuşadası Scene
Barlar Sokağı (Beer St/Pub Lane) has the greatest concentration of pubs and discos, and appeals especially to young British people. Beer flows and the decibel count remains high until well into the morning. The pubs and discos in the Kale district, the old part of town, are more interesting in appearance at least, with small courtyards turned into bars and dancing floors. She, Ecstasy, Green Bar and Another Bar are some of the more popular joints.

Pubs & Bars

Northern Aegean

Çanakkale

Akol Roof Bar
The Roof Bar on the top floor of the Akol hotel (► 100) is the best place to enjoy a cocktail while watching the sun set over the Dardanelles. Depending on your taste, the live popular music will either add to or detract from the overall experience.

✉ Akol Hotel, Kordonboyu
🕐 6PM–late ☎ (0286) 217 9456

Alesta Bar
There is not really a great deal to do in Çanakkale at night and this cosy little bar offers some diversion. It opens early in the evening but only around midnight does the place tend to liven up with music and conviviality. It's certainly worth a visit and centrally located in town.

✉ Yalı Caddesi ☎ (0286) 217 0839 🕐 6PM–early morning

Çeşme

Lowry's Irish Pub
The owner of this popular bar is actually Irish so this is not just another bogus Irish theme pub. There is live music most nights and drinks are served inside or at the small garden pool outside. Turkish and Irish-style food is available. The Zee Gold Hotel on the same street has a less authentic Irish-theme pub downstairs.

✉ İzmir Caddesi, Ilica ☎ (0232) 723 0425 🕐 mid-morning–late
🚌 Dolmuş/minibus to Çeşme

İzmir

Windows on the Bay
The 31st floor of the Hilton hotel provides panoramic views of the largest city on the Aegean coast and its splendid bay. From 6 to 9PM business people unwind here with drinks after work, while from 11PM to closing time the atmosphere is much more fun, with middle-of-the-road pop music played by international bands. There is no cover charge but an affordable minimum charge at night.

✉ Gazi Osman Paşa Bulvarı ☎ (0232) 441 6060 🕐 11AM–2:30AM 🚌 61–63, 116, 110, 112, 150

Kuşadası

Rhodes
Depending on the time of your visit, this can be a relatively quiet place for cocktails and conversation. The Mexican Bar next door attracts a noisy crowd, and a few doors up the Captain's House is a large café and bar with live music but no dancing.

✉ Atatürk Caddesi ☎ (0256) 614 6362 🕐 mid-morning–late

Selçuk

Don Kişot
There are basically only two bars in Selçuk with a bit of life and atmosphere. Don Kişot is small, with a misguided colour scheme, but lively enough. The other bar is the Pink Bar, larger and a little more sophisticated, just around the corner.

✉ Sokak 1005 6/A 🕐 mid-morning–late

Southern Aegean

Bodrum

Ora

A cavernous, ancient-looking building that usually manages to fill every inch of its floor space with revellers. This is one of the most popular bars in Bodrum and while the slogan of 'the bar where you can dance on the tables' is not always taken literally, it gives a good idea of the atmosphere and appeal of the place.

✉ **Dr Alim Bey Caddesi 19/21** ☎ **(0252) 614 63903** 🕐 **mid-morning–late**

'Quick Drink Street'

This is the literal translation of Tektekçiler Sokak, a narrow street filled with small wooden chairs and the sound of Turkish music played on traditional instruments. The idea is that one passes through this street, stopping for ten minutes or so to enjoy a drink and take in the music and singing, then moving on to somewhere else. To find the street, take the first right after passing the Ora (see above) pub.

✉ **Tektekçiler Sokak** 🕐 **Early to late evening**

Fethiye & Hisarönü

Boozey Bar

This is a no-frills bar with taped music and a snooker table that is popular with English visitors. The place never really goes over the top but can be relied on to remain convivial and...well, boozy.

✉ **Hisarönü** ☎ **(0252)–616 6726** 🕐 **11AM–late**

🚌 *Dolmuş*/minibus to Fethiye

Ottoman Café

It is a little surprising there aren't more pubs like this one along the coast. The interior re-creates, with some imagination, an Ottoman-style atmosphere with the help of antique copper pots adorning the walls and Turkish folk music. The place is sometimes taken over by package groups brought here by tour operators, but it can make a relaxing venue during the afternoon or early evening.

✉ **Karagözler Caddesi 3/B Fethiye** ☎ **(0252) 612 1148** 🕐 **10AM–4PM**

Clubs & Discos

Northern Aegean

Çeşme

Korfez

In the restaurant of the same name with free entry and mainly attracting the 20–35 age group for live music, mostly Turkish pop and international songs. Other discos include the Le Garage, Disco Viking and the Fly Inn.

✉ **Yalı Caddesi 12** ☎ **(0232) 712 6718** 🕐 **Midnight–4AM**

Kuşadası

Emperor

This is just one of the many discos that rub shoulders with 'Irish' and 'English' pubs in Kuşadası's Bar Street. The atmosphere is loud and racy, and the occasional local is heavily outnumbered by British holidaymakers determined to have a good time.

✉ **Barlar Sokaği (Beer St) 21** ☎ **(0256) 612 2575** 🕐 **8PM–early morning**

The Marmaris Scene

Marmaris also has its Beer Street/Pub Lane quarter where pubs and discos rub shoulders with one another. Predominantly British in character, the area is very noisy but friendly, with Turkish bands playing Western pop music. Check out, for starters, The Green House, Horizon, Casablanca and the Blue Moon.

Diving

In Kuşadası the Grand Blue Sky hotel (▶ 101) is home to the Aquaventure Diving Centre ☎ (0256) 144479 with one-day demonstration dives, 2-day introductory courses and 5-day PADI courses available. The British-managed European Diving Centre in Içmler ☎ (0252) 4554733 is one of the most professional companies offering certificated diving courses.

Club 33

Occupies a central spot, right across Bird Island. A fairly good sound and light system, a decent bar and DJs.

✉ **Bird Island** ☎ (0256) 612 4723 🕐 7PM–early morning

Southern Aegean

Bodrum

Jazz Café

This place gets off to a slow start with jazz music early in the evening, but as midnight approaches the music changes and the dancing gets going. Very popular and very lively, even at 4AM.

✉ **Paşatarlası Caddesi 9** ☎ (0252) 614 66341 🕐 7PM–5AM

Halikarnas

This legendary outdoor disco is the number one hot spot in Bodrum. The laser and light show, usually around midnight, is spectacular and other diversions come in the form of exotic-looking belly dancers and leather-clad professional dancing groups. The DJs are very good and usually include a well-known personality from Britain.

✉ **Cumhuriyet Caddesi** ☎ (0252) 316 8000 🕐 8PM–early morning

M&M Dancing

This very large indoor disco is one of Bodrum's top night spots. The light shows are worth catching. The DJs keep the rock music going and maintain a very upbeat atmosphere. Occasional theme nights.

✉ **Dr Alim Bey Caddesi** ☎ (0252) 316 2725 🕐 7PM–4AM

Fethiye

Disco Marina

This lively disco attracts young Turkish people as well as overseas visitors. Not as sophisticated as the Bodrum and Marmaris discos, but enlivened by professional dance routines.

✉ **Yat Mimanı** ☎ (0252) 614 9861 🕐 9PM–early morning

Yes!

Run by a Turkish-English couple and successfully attracting a mixture of Turkish and European visitors. Entry is free, happy hour is from 9 to midnight. Music livens up after 11PM with oldies as well as current favourites. Occasional theme nights and dancing shows include belly dancers.

✉ **Cumhuriyet Caddesi 9** ☎ (0252) 614 9289 🕐 8PM–4AM

Music Factory

This is currently the most popular disco for the younger people in Fethiye. The dancing starts around 11PM. There are occasional shows, and professional dancers make effective use of the balcony that surrounds the dance floor.

✉ **Hamam Sokak 29** ☎ (0252) 612 3778 🕐 7:30 PM–4 AM

Marmaris & Içmeler

Joy

This is a well-established disco in Içmeler and its circular shape makes it easy to identify, on the right side of the main road as you come into Içmeler from Marmaris.

✉ **Içmeler** ☎ (0252) 455 3302 🕐 11PM–3AM 🚌 *Dolmuş/* minibus to Marmaris

Turkish Baths & Massage

Turkish Bath & Massage

Turkey's fine tradition of a cleansing and sociable bathtime goes back to the influence of the Romans, and a visit to a traditional bath house (*hamam*) is a memorable part of any visit to Turkey. After depositing clothes in a locker you don a wrap (*peştamal*) and proceed to the main bath area, where an attendant delivers a refreshing body scrub of varying degrees of intensity, depending on the establishment. Rinsing and shampooing follows, in preparation for the massage. The massage should be on the great slab of marble that dominates the centre of any *hamam*. In a very tourist-oriented *hamam* the experience may prove disappointingly mild, perhaps because the masseur thinks you might not recover from the full, highly invigorating treatment. If the masseur uses only soap, rather than oil, for the massage then it is not the real thing.

The traditional *hamam* has separate days of the week for male and female customers and will use male and female masseurs respectively.

Northern Aegean

Çeşme

Turkish Bath
Advertisements for this prosaically named *hamam* promise 'a fantastic time and exotic massage with professional stuff'.
 Çarşı Caddesi ☎ (0232) 712 8311 🕐 9AM–9PM

Kuşadası

Belediye
Situated across from the old mosque and featuring traditional mixed bathing.
✉ Yildirmit Caddesi, Kuşadası ☎ (0256) 6141219 🕐 9AM–9PM

Selçuk
The *hamam* is in the centre of town, next door to the police station. Mixed bathing and a soft massage.
✉ Sokak 2002 ☎ (0232) 892 6198 🕐 Mid-morning to 10PM

Southern Aegean

Bodrum

Hamam
This is a more traditional *hamam* than you might expect for Bodrum. Wednesday and Saturday afternoons are for women only.
✉ Dere Umucra Sokak 🕐 8AM–5PM

Fethiye
Although the *hamam* itself dates back to the 16th century, this is a touristy establishment and one that most Turkish people would turn up their noses at, though there is a barber on the premises.
✉ Hamam Sokak 20 ☎ (0252) 614 9318 🕐 7AM–midnight

Marmaris

Sultan
Unashamedly aimed at the tourist market, with women-only and men-only baths as well as a mixed one and a choice of massages.
✉ Taşlık Centre ☎ (0252) 413 6850 🕐 8AM–midnight

Wrestling

In early summer there are slippery wrestling contests in which oil-covered opponents attempt to keep each other pinned down on their backs for a set time. In winter months, especially in the area around İzmir and Ephesus, there are camel-wrestling events that provide popular entertainment for young and old alike.

What's On When

Religious Holidays & Festivals

Only a few special days occur at the same time every year in Turkey because they are calculated according to the Muslim lunar calendar. *Kurban Bayramı* is a festival of sacrifice commemorating Abraham's willingness to sacrifice his son Isaac. It is marked by the sacrifice of millions of lambs across the country and the distribution of the meat to those in need. During the month of Ramadan, usually around **January/February**, Muslims do not eat, drink or smoke between sunrise and sunset, but this should not cause a problem for anyone travelling along the Aegean coast. The end of Ramadan is celebrated by a festival (*İeker Bayramı*), marked by family get-togethers and the exchanging of sweets.

Local Events

Mid-January to **late February** is the time to watch for camel wrestling in the Selçuk and Denizli areas.
15 March in Çanakkale is usually marked by special events, commemorating the 1915 victory at sea.
Mid-April sees the İzmir Film Festival, an international festival featuring foreign releases in their own languages.
Late April to **mid-May** sees the Ephesus Festival in and around Selçuk. Music and dancing events take place, although the staging of events in the ancient theatre is currently being affected by the restoration programme.
First week in May is International Yacht Week in Marmaris and different regatta and arts events take place. There is also a yacht race during the first week of November.
June sees a watersports festival in Foçça and different cultural events are staged. International offshore racing takes place between Istanbul and İzmir.
Mid-June–early July is the time of the International İzmir Festival, with events also taking place at Selçuk and Ephesus.
Early July sees Çeşme host a Song and Music competition.
August/September sees İzmir hosting its annual International Trade Fair. The practical result of this for non-commercial visitors is that the better hotels, and even restaurants, will be heavily booked.
Early September sees the Selçuk Festival, featuring Turkish folk dances and musical events.

Market Days

It is always worth asking at the local tourist office about where and when the weekly market is held. Such market days are important to Turkish people living in the countryside, and the local town will be visibly busier with the influx. Usually there will be an area in town set apart for stalls and, although the merchandise is not targeted at tourists, the scene is still a lively one and worth a visit. Kuşadası is an exception in that the two weekly markets (Tuesday and Friday) are also aimed at tourists. You can get more information at the local tourist office.

Practical Matters

Above: *a proud taxi-driver in Çanakkale; not all taxis are looked after so well*
Right: *in other places the pace of travel is slower*

TIME DIFFERENCES

GMT
12 noon

Turkey West Coast →
2PM

Germany →
1PM

USA (NY) ←
7AM

Netherlands →
1PM

Spain →
1PM

WHAT YOU NEED

- ● Required
- ○ Suggested
- ▲ Not required

	UK	Germany	USA	Netherlands	Spain
Passport/National Identity Card	●	●	●	●	●
Visa (obtainable on arrival)	●	▲	●	●	●
Onward or Return Ticket	○	○	○	○	○
Health Inoculations	▲	▲	▲	▲	▲
Health Documentation (Health, ➤ 123)	▲	▲	▲	▲	▲
Travel Insurance	○	○	○	○	○
Driving Licence (EU or International)	●	●	●	●	●
Car Insurance Certificate (if own car)	●	●	●	●	●
Car registration document (if own car)	●	●	●	●	●

WHEN TO GO

Turkey's West Coast

☐ High season
☐ Low season

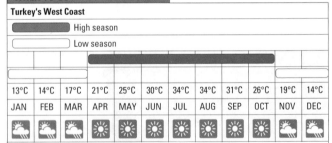

JAN	FEB	MAR	APR	MAY	JUN	JUL	AUG	SEP	OCT	NOV	DEC
13°C	14°C	17°C	21°C	25°C	30°C	34°C	34°C	31°C	26°C	19°C	14°C

 Sun

 Sunshine & showers

TOURIST OFFICES

In the UK
Turkish Information Office
First Floor, Egyptian House
170–3 Piccadilly
London WIV 9DD
☎ (0171) 355 4207
Fax: (0171) 491 0773

In the USA
Turkish Information Office
821 United Nations Plaza
New York
NY 10017
☎ 212/687 2194
Fax: 212/599 7568

1717 Massachusetts Ave
NW
Suite 306
Washington DC
DC 20036
☎ 202/429 9844

POLICE 155

JANDARMA (IN COUNTRY AREAS) 156

FIRE 110

AMBULANCE 112

WHEN YOU ARE THERE

ARRIVING

Turkish Airlines has scheduled flights to İzmir via Istanbul from major European cities, and Cyprus Turkish Airlines flies direct to İzmir from London, but charter flights are much cheaper. Ferry services operate from Italy, and from many Greek islands. International flights also serve Bodrum and Dalaman.

Adnan Menderes Airport Kilometres to İzmir	**Journey times**	
	🚇	N/A
	🚌	30 minutes
25 kilometres	🚕	20 minutes

Dalaman Airport Kilometres to Fethiye	**Journey times**	
	🚇	N/A
	🚌	60 minutes
50 kilometres	🚕	45 minutes

MONEY

Turkey's currency is the lira, abbreviated as TL and issued in notes of 50,000, 100,000, 250,000, 500,000, 1,000,000 and 5,000,000. Coins come in 2500, 5000, 10,000, 25,000 and 50,000TL. Travellers' cheques are accepted in banks and exchange offices but a commission of 2–3 per cent is levied. Foreign currency in cash can be exchanged without any commission being charged. Eurocheques and credit cards are accepted. Changing money in banks can take a long time; it is better to use the post office (PTT) or the money exchange offices in the main towns.

TIME

 Local time is 2 hours ahead of Greenwich Mean Time (GMT+2) but daylight saving (GMT+3) operates between late March and late September.

CUSTOMS

 YES

Limited amounts of alcohol, cigarettes and coffee may be brought into the country.

Liquor (wine or spirits): 5 litres
Cigarettes: 200
Cigars: 50
Tobacco: 200g
Coffee: 1.5kg

A record of any expensive items such as a video camera or laptop computer may be made in your passport to ensure that it is brought back out of the country. Any item worth over £10,000 must be entered in your passport. Cellular telephones must be accompanied by certification of ownership and will be recorded in your passport.

 NO

Drugs, firearms, ammunition, offensive weapons, obscene material and unlicensed animals.

119

EMBASSIES AND CONSULATES

UK	Germany	USA	Netherlands	Spain
(0232) 463 5151	(0232) 421 6995	(0232) 421 3643	(0232) 463 4960	(0232) 489 7936

WHEN YOU ARE THERE

TOURIST OFFICES

- Bodrum
  Bariş Meydanı 48
  ☎ (0252) 316 1091

- Çanakkale
  Next to main dock
  ☎ (0217) 0286 1187

- Fethiye
  İskele Karşısı 1
  ☎ (0252) 614 1527

- İzmir
  418 Atatürk Caddesi
  ☎ (0232) 422 0207

- Kuşadası
  Liman Caddesi
  ☎ (0256) 614 1103

- Marmaris
  İskele Meydanı 2
  ☎ (0252) 412 1035

- Selçuk
  Atatürk Mah.,
  EfesMüzesi Karşısı 23
  ☎ (0232) 892 1328

There are also tourist offices in most towns of interest: see individual entries for addresses and telephone numbers.

NATIONAL HOLIDAYS

J	F	M	A	M	J	J	A	S	O	N	D
1			1	1			1		1		

1 Jan	New Year's Day
23 Apr	Independence Day
19 May	Atatürk Commemoration Youth and Sports Day
30 Aug	Commemoration of the Turkish victory over the Greeks in 1922
29 Oct	Commemoration of the Proclamation of the Republic in 1923

Moveable Holidays
Islamic holidays, the dates of which change from year to year, are also recognised in most of Turkey (see ► 116).

OPENING HOURS

○ Shops	● Archaeological Sites
● Offices	○ Museums/Monuments
● Banks	● Pharmacies

| 8AM | 9AM | 10AM | NOON | 1PM | 2PM | 4PM | 5PM | 7PM |

☐ Day	☐ Midday
☐ Evening	

In addition to the times shown above, shops in tourist areas may open earlier and stay open for much longer, sometimes until midnight, every day of the week. Banks are closed on Saturdays and Sundays. Museums are usually closed on Mondays.

DRIVE ON THE
RIGHT

TOILETS
CHARGE

PUBLIC TRANSPORT

 Internal Flights Turkish Airlines operate domestic flights connecting Istanbul, Ankara and most of Turkey's major cities with the airports at Dalaman, İzmir and Bodrum.

 Trains There is a very limited, and usually very slow train service covering a small area of western Turkey, and few visitors use it. From İzmir, trains run to Selçuk, Denizli and Manisa. For reservations ☎ (0232) 484 5353.

 Buses Buses are the most popular and practical means of getting around. Fares are inexpensive and the service is usually very reliable and professional. Tickets can be purchased at the bus station (*otogar*), in advance, and sometimes on the actual bus if you board after the starting point. Smoking is not allowed on buses.

 Boat Trips The best way to see the coastline, and to reach otherwise inaccessible coves, is by boat. In all the major resorts, boat operators will be found at the harbour. Longer cruises with a crew, lasting 3–7 days, are especially popular from Bodrum and Marmaris. Ferries to Greek islands are commonplace.

 Dolmuş/minibus A *dolmuş* is a shared taxi. You pay according to the distance travelled and can get on or off anywhere along the route. For most travel in the region, the *dolmuş* is a minibus and you pay on board. For local travel between villages or small towns, it is the best means of transport.

CAR RENTAL

 Leading international car rental companies have offices in İzmir and some of the larger resorts. Many visitors book their car hire in advance from their home country. Drivers must be over 21 and have a valid driving licence.

TAXIS

 Taxis are usually yellow, and can be hailed from the pavement or from ranks in the major resorts. Fares are metered and the cost is reasonable for short journeys. Fares double between midnight and 6AM.

DRIVING

 Speed limit on motorways: **120kph**

 Speed limit in open areas: **90kph**

 Speed limit in towns: **50kph**

 Seat belts must be worn in front seats at all times and in rear seats where fitted.

 There is a total ban on alcohol when driving. Random tests are quite common and police will issue on-the-spot fines.

 Petrol stations sell super and normal petrol (*benzin*), and diesel (*mazot*). Unleaded petrol (*kursunsuz*) is available in towns and larger petrol stations. Credit cards are accepted. Service stations often have good toilets and are full service.

 If you break down driving your own car, call the Turkish Touring and Automobile Club (☎ Istanbul (0212) 282 8140; fax (0212) 282 8042). If your car is hired, follow the instructions you were given when hiring the vehicle.

PERSONAL SAFETY

The everyday police force in towns have blue uniforms. There are special tourist police in the major resorts who look the same but who should be able to speak some English and/or German.
To help prevent crime:
• Do not carry more cash than you need
• Do not leave valuables on the beach or at the poolside
• Use safe boxes in your hotel
• Never leave anything of value in your car

Police assistance:
☎ **155**
from any call box

TELEPHONES

Phonecards are available in 30, 60, 100, 120 and 180 units. You can make phone calls from the local post office (PTT), where phonecards may also be purchased. Phone booths in the street are not difficult to find. To call for directory assistance dial 118 and for the international operator dial 115.

International Dialling Codes	
From Turkey to:	
UK:	**00 44**
Germany:	**00 49**
USA & Canada:	**00 1**
Netherlands:	**00 31**
Spain:	**00 34**

POST

Post offices (PTT) are easily recognisable by a black-on-yellow logo. In the major resorts and larger towns the main PTT will stay open for phone calls until midnight. Open: 8AM–7/8PM. Closed: Sat PM and Sun. Stamps are usually available where postcards are sold.

ELECTRICITY

The power supply in Turkey is 220 volts.

Sockets take two round pin plugs but there are two sizes in use. Bring your own adaptor. Travellers from the USA will need a transformer.

TIPS/GRATUITIES

Yes ✓ No ✗		
Restaurants (service not inc)	✓	10%
Cafés/bar (if service not inc.)	✓	change
Tour Guides	✓	100,000–250,000TL
Hairdressers	✓	change
Taxis	✓	round up fair
Chambermaids	✓	
Hotel porters	✓	
Cloakroom attendants/toilets	✓	
Petrol-pump attendants	✓	

What to photograph: archaeological sites, fishing villages and attractive harbours, sunsets.
What not to photograph: anything to do with the military.
When to photograph: The summer sun can be powerful the height of the day, making photographs sometimes appear too 'flat'; early morning or late evening is a better time.
Where to buy films: Film and camera batteries are readily available from tourist shops in the main resorts.

HEALTH

Insurance
Arrange travel insurance in your home country before arriving in Turkey. Turkey is not a member of the EU, so EU visitors cannot obtain free medical treatment.

Dental Services
Dental treatment must be paid for. Check your travel insurance to see whether, and to what extent, dental treatment is covered.

Sun Advice
The sunniest and hottest months are July, August and September, with an average of twelve hours of sunshine and temperatures in the low 30s°C. During these months especially you should avoid the midday sun and use a strong sunblock.

Drugs
Prescription and non-prescription drugs and medicines are available from pharmacies (*eczane*). They are able to dispense many drugs that would normally be available only on prescription in many countries.

Safe Water
Tap water is generally safe to drink, though it can be heavily chlorinated and unpleasant. Mineral water is inexpensive and is sold either fizzy (*maden suyu*) or flat (*memba suyu*).

CONCESSIONS

Students/Youth
Holders of an International Student Identity Card (ISIC) may be able to obtain some concessions on travel and entrance fees. There is the occasional hostel where an ISIC card is helpful. Inexpensive accommodation is also available in pensions (*pansiyons*).

CLOTHING SIZES

Turkey	UK	Europe	USA	
46	36	46	36	
48	38	48	38	
50	40	50	40	Suits
52	42	52	42	
54	44	54	44	
56	46	56	46	
41	7	41	8	
42	7.5	42	8.5	
43	8.5	43	9.5	Shoes
44	9.5	44	10.5	
45	10.5	45	11.5	
46	11	46	12	
37	14.5	37	14.5	
38	15	38	15	
39/40	15.5	39/40	15.5	Shirts
41	16	41	16	
42	16.5	42	16.5	
43	17	43	17	
36	8	34	6	
38	10	36	8	
40	12	38	10	Dresses
42	14	40	12	
44	16	42	14	
46	18	44	16	
38	4.5	38	6	
38	5	38	6.5	
39	5.5	39	7	Shoes
39	6	39	7.5	
40	6.5	40	8	
41	7	41	8.5	

WHEN DEPARTING

- Confirm your flight departure one or two days before leaving.
- Remaining Turkish currency is of little use and small amounts will not easily be exchanged in your own country.
- Departure tax is usually paid for when you purchase your ticket but check that this is so in your case.

LANGUAGE

Turkish is not an easy language to pick up, but happily many people in Turkey speak English and/or German or French. However, even the most basic attempt at uttering a few words in Turkish will always be greatly appreciated by Turks. Since Atatürk abolished the Arabic script, Turkish is written in the Latin alphabet, but several letters are pronounced differently. *ay* = igh as in night *c* = j *ç* = ch *ğ/y* = silent, lengthening the preceding vowel *i* = e as in scene *j* = zh *ö* = ur *ş* = sh *ü* = ew

hotel	*otel*	bath	*banyo*
pension	*pansiyon*	shower	*duş*
single room	*tek kişilik oda*	toilet	*tuvalet*
double room	*iki kişilik oda*	hot water	*sıcak su*
one night	*bir gecelik*	key	*anahtar*
reservation	*reservasyon*	lift	*asansör*
room service	*oda servisi*	sea view	*deniz manzarası*
towel	*havlu*	reception	*resepsiyon*

bank	*banka*	credit card	*kredi kart*
exchange office	*kambiyo bürosu*	exchange rate	*döviz kuru*
post office	*PTT or postane*	commission	*komisyon ücreti*
stamp	*pul*	charge	
cheque	*çeki*	cashier	*kasiyer*
traveller's	*seyahat çeki*	change	*bozuk para*
cheque		foreign currency	*doviz*

restaurant	*okanta/restoran*	fruit	*meyva*
bill	*hesap*	bread	*ekmek*
breakfast	*kahvaltı*	beer	*bira*
appetisers/	*meze/*	wine	*şarap*
vegetable in	*zeytinyağlılar*	ice	*buz*
olive oil		water	*su*
dessert	*tatlı*	mineral water	*maden suyu*
yoghurt drink	*ayran*	coffee	*kahve*
tea	*çay*	milk	*süt*

aeroplane	*uçak*	return	*gidiş-dönüş*
airport	*havaalanı*	port	*liman*
train station	*istasyon*	car	*araba*
bus	*otobüs*	taxi	*taksi*
bus station	*otogar*	how do I get to...?	*...'a/e nasil*
boat	*vapur/feribot*		*giderim?*
ferry landing	*iskele*	how far is..?	*...ne kadar uzak?*
a ticket to...	*...'a bir bilet*	where is...?	*...nerede?*

yes	*evet*	goodbye	*güle güle* (said by
no	*hayır, yok*		the one staying)
please	*lütfen*	good morning	*günaydin*
thank you	*teşekkür ederim,*	good afternoon	*iyi günler*
	mersi, sağol	goodnight	*iyi geceler*
hello	*merhaba*	sorry	*pardon*
goodbye	*allahaısmarladık*	how much?	*ne kadar/kaça?*
	(said by the one	open/closed	*açık/kapalı*
	leaving)	excuse me	*özür dilerim*
you're welcome	*bir şey değil*	where?	*nerede?*

INDEX

Acknowledgements

Sean Sheehan would like to thank;

Peter Espley at the Turkish Tourist Office in London, Suat Oral in Bodrum, Hale Özakar in Küsadasi, Sihel Romano in Marmaris, Sean Walwyn in İzmir, Hakan Ergir in Selçuk and all the kind people in the tourist offices along the Aegean coast who patiently helped with his enquiries.

The Automobile Association wishes to thank the following photographers and libraries for their assistance in the preparation of this book.

J ALLAN CASH PHOTOLIBRARY 85, 90; MARY EVANS PICTURE LIBRARY 14b; MRI BANKERS GUIDE TO FOREIGN CURRENCY 119; ROBERT HARDING PICTURE LIBRARY 68, 77; INTERNATIONAL PHOTOBANK front cover (c) Kemer, man; NATURE PHOTOGRAPHERS LTD 12 (K Carlson), 40 (P Craig-Cooper), 49 (P R Sterry); PICTURES COLOUR LIBRARY 62b; SPECTRUM COLOUR LIBRARY 10/1, 26b, 89b

The remaining photographs are held in the Association's own photo library (AA PHOTO LIBRARY) and were taken by Jean-François Pin with the exception of the following pages: 82b taken by Steve Day; 5b, 6b, 6c, 8c, 9c, 11, 13, 15a, 16a, 17a, 18a, 19a, 20a, 20b, 21a, 22a, 22b, 23a, 22/3, 24a, 25a, 26a, 31c, 32b, 36b, 39b, 41b, 44, 45, 46, 47b, 48, 50, 51a, 52b, 55b, 60b, 64/5, 65, 69b, 71a, 74, 75, 76, 80a, 81b, 83, 86b, 86c, 88, 91a, 92, 93, 94, 95, 96, 97, 98, 99, 100, 101, 102, 103, 104, 105, 106, 107, 108, 109, 110, 111, 112, 113, 114, 115, 116, 117b, 122c taken by Paul Kenward; 15b, 16b, 24b taken by Dario Mitideri and 70b/ 87b which were taken by Tony Souter.

Copy editor: Antonia Hebbert   **Page layout** Barfoot Design

Dear Essential Traveller

**Your comments, opinions and recommendations are very
important to us. So please help us to improve our travel
guides by taking a few minutes to complete this simple
questionnaire.**

*You do not need a stamp (unless posted outside the UK). If you do not want to cut this page
from your guide, then photocopy it or write your answers on a plain sheet of paper.*

Send to: **The Editor, AA World Travel Guides,
FREEPOST SCE 4598, Basingstoke RG21 4GY.**

Your recommendations...

We always encourage readers' recommendations for restaurants, nightlife
or shopping – if your recommendation is used in the next edition of the
guide, we will send you a *FREE* AA *Essential* Guide of your choice.
Please state below the establishment name, location and your reasons
for recommending it.

_____

_____

_____

_____

Please send me **AA *Essential*** _____
(*see list of titles inside the front cover*)

About this guide...

Which title did you buy?
    AA *Essential* _____
Where did you buy it? _____
When? _ _ / _ _

Why did you choose an AA *Essential* Guide? _____

_____

_____

_____

_____

Did this guide meet your expectations?
    Exceeded ☐   Met all ☐   Met most ☐   Fell below ☐
    Please give your reasons_____

_____

_____

_____

continued on next page...

Were there any aspects of this guide that you particularly liked? _____
_____
_____
_____

Is there anything we could have done better? _____
_____
_____
_____
_____

About you...

Name (Mr/Mrs/Ms) _____
    Address _____
    _____
    _____ Postcode _____
    Daytime tel nos _____

Which age group are you in?
    Under 25 ☐ 25–34 ☐ 35–44 ☐ 45–54 ☐ 55–64 ☐ 65+ ☐

How many trips do you make a year?
    Less than one ☐ One ☐ Two ☐ Three or more ☐

Are you an AA member? Yes ☐ No ☐

About your trip...

When did you book? m m / y y   When did you travel? m m / y y
How long did you stay? _____
Was it for business or leisure? _____
Did you buy any other travel guides for your trip?
    If yes, which ones? _____
    _____

Thank you for taking the time to complete this questionnaire. Please send
    it to us as soon as possible, and remember, you do not need a stamp
    (unless posted outside the UK).

Happy Holidays!